The Folly
of Repetition or
The Wisdom
of Remembrance

30 Crucial Neglected
Lessons of History

Craig Chalquist

World Soul Books
654 Center Street
Walnut Creek, CA 94595

Printed in the United States of America
ISBN 978-0-9826279-0-7

Cover photograph by Craig Chalquist.

Visit the author's web site at Chalquist.com.

Table of Contents

DEDICATION

To all who struggle soulfully and ceaselessly against the
archons of human history.

Introduction:
Remembering, Not Repeating

Most semi-educated survivors of a contemporary public education can recognize the quotation, "Those who cannot remember the past are condemned to repeat it," even if they do not know it came from George Santayana's *The Life of Reason*. Those unable to learn from what has happened (as the philosopher explains in that section of his book) are akin to "children and barbarians."

This alone should suffice to justify exposure to the humanities. Who wants to go on repeating the same old mistakes? Would George W. Bush have postured so brazenly upon the deck of an aircraft carrier, a huge MISSION ACCOMPLISHED banner behind him signaling the supposed U.S. victory in Iraq, had he known the last words of another George, name of Custer, at Little Bighorn?—"Hurrah, boys, now we have 'em!" Would agribusiness managers in California's Central Valley continue to monocrop and irrigate the land to death if they truly understood why the salt-choked Fertile Crescent is no longer fertile? Why were Americans surprised when big banks whose irresponsibility had wrecked the economy used untracked bailout funds to enrich executive officers, buy out competitors, and pay out huge bonuses?

Because the humanities (and education in general) attract so little funding in my country in comparison with incarceration, warfare, lobbying, and petroleum subsidization, those who want to learn something relevant from the past must do their reading beyond the official curriculum. That is the primary reason for this little book.

The question around which the book turns is this: **What unlearned lessons from history do we go on repeating?** Thirty of the most urgent are covered herein: urgent because of the destructive effects of failing to learn them. Each chapter describes a key historical example of an unlearned lesson and ends with a one-sentence summary in bold print.

Unlearned lessons are usually unpleasant, which is why they go unlearned. It may be, however, that psychological adulthood can be defined as a capacity for facing that which we do not want to hear. The ruler who kills the messenger, the boss who demotes the whistleblower, and the armchair patriot who shouts down repeated warnings about the ongoing loss of civil liberties share something important in common: developmental arrest.

Causing incalculable misery to ourselves and our planet, these thirty unlearned lessons prevent us from maturing emotionally, from evolving culturally, from getting along with each other, from making constructive decisions, from enriching our possibilities for community, from healing our relationship to the declining natural world, from guarding business and politics from ruthless exploitation, and, in short, from being touched by what President Lincoln referred to in his first inaugural speech as "the better angels of our nature." We need those angels now more than ever.

As an educator, I have often seen that when people understand the consequences of past mistakes, they tend to *remember* them rather than *repeat* them. This fact carries huge implications for personal and social change once we realize how much of today's mayhem, disorder, stupidity, and harm results directly from such preventable mistakes.

Equipped with this knowledge, we can face squarely up to perils like poverty, anomie, plutocracy, corruption, pollution, war, paranoia, and ignorance and realize another crucial truth forgotten by every society that perishes instead of redesigning itself:

Things really don't have to be this way.

1 - Mesopotamia:
War and "Human Nature"

Are we fated to be warlike?

10,000 years ago, our species underwent the deepest cultural transformation of its existence. We have been living with the consequences ever since.

10,000 years might sound like a long stretch, but it represents a mere 5% of the lifespan of Homo sapiens. That lifespan in turn occupies only a tiny fraction of millions of years of evolutionary prehistory. 10,000 years: a whisper, an eyeblink, a mere blip in the radar screen of organic time as life on Earth measures it out.

10,000 years ago, the last Ice Age was in full retreat. In fact, a drought warmed what is now southern Iraq so much that large game and many useful plants were withering and dying. Normally gathering and hunting provided local people with enough to eat and wear, but that time was coming to an end.

As food supplies fell off, an alternative presented itself.

Prehistoric human beings had probably always stored what food they managed to gather, but here in what would become known as the Fertile Crescent, edible grains were extravagantly abundant. Perhaps some scattering of cereals grown from seeds escaped from a leaky storage bin gave someone a bright idea; in any case, here in Mesopotamia (today southern Iraq and Iran) is where single crops, not the blends and mixtures nature prefers, began to be grown systematically.

Crops grown this way can often feed more people—sometimes many more people—than those taken from the ground more or less at random. But they demand special conditions in exchange for the nourishment they offer. Someone must stay near them and watch over them, a fact that hardens slowly into villages and, eventually, urban centers. Some of the crop tenders must be farmers, of course; others, accountants to keep track of what's grown; still others, traders, and craftsmen to invent new containers and carts and other food-related technologies. Priests to bless the crops, soldiers to guard them, officers to command and organize the soldiers; writers, mathematicians, ranchers, police....

In other words, this relatively simple act of planting crops leads over time to what we now think of as urban civilization. DNA analysis shows that most Europeans and North Americans are descended from Fertile Crescent farmers who spread their cultures and technologies around the world as similar developments sprouted in other places: South America, India, China, Egypt, Africa.

Of course, every large-scale development brings problems, carries risks, casts a shadow. With the rise of urban life, centralized power, authoritarianism, institutionalized religion, patriarchy, and warfare slowly began to infiltrate, and then to dominate, human affairs. When Sargon I assembled his armed Akkadian dynasty in 2,334 BC, empire as a psychology, a philosophy, a goal, and a way of life entered the lists of history and has remained the dominant gladiator ever since.

Conquest requires rationalizations to ease the conqueror's conscience. Empire psychology's most popular one has always been that war is an unalterable expression of human nature. However, before 10,000 years ago, nobody had reason to conquer anything. Tribal skirmishes and local violence recede into the mists of prehistory, having undoubtedly been features of human life for time out of mind, but according to the archaeological record to date, institutionalized warfare, with commanders, officers, racks of weapons, and organized troops, flares into being only 10,000 years ago and really picks up only eight to seven thousand years ago.

Even now, organized warfare remains unknown in cultures that rely on horticulture rather than monocrop agriculture. Among the Sami, the oldest indigenous horticulturalists and reindeer herders in Europe, no record exists of any having organized or commanded armies. When Cortes came to Mexico, he beat the Aztecs in part because they fought their battles man-on-man, without strategy or unified tactics. Native people fight to set boundaries or to defend themselves. By contrast, large troop formations are designed to exterminate opponents, to conquer and rule over territory and occupants.

The conclusion is clear: War, as historian and urban planner Lewis Mumford explained, is a cultural institution. Nature, including human nature, tends to be self-correcting until interfered with. Cycles of predation, self-defense, and even animal infanticide and mutilation of prey remain different in their aims and passions from the systematized paranoia and hatred required to wipe out entire populations.

We should not romanticize the goodness of human nature, but neither should we sell it short. People raised in safe and enriching settings that offer plenty of education, support, and love tend not to become exploitive, aggressive, or antisocial adults. By contrast, those raised where hypocrisy, aggression, competition, and bullying are the "eat or be eaten" norms are likely to grow up twisted, like plants with stunted roots.

Who is most vested in selling war as eternal in addition to the paranoid personality projecting its own violent impulses onto convenient scapegoats (see Chapter 21)? Predictably, the most predatory among governments, businesses, syndicates, armies, and religions seeking the illusion of secure immortality by being first in line to govern. In this they resemble 19th-Century monopoly industrialists who claimed that people were at heart selfish capitalists.

The historical lesson? Beware of cynics devoid of faith in humanity:

Human nature is cast as warlike and depraved primarily by those who benefit from repressive programs to control it.

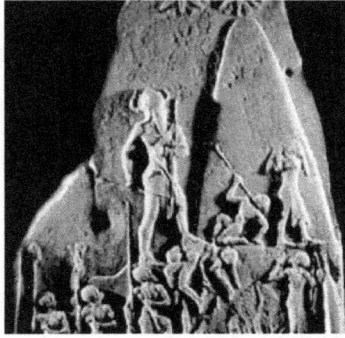

2 - Sumer:
The Future of Empire

By 5,000 years ago, the rising state of Sumer in southern Mesopotamia had applied Fertile Crescent farming techniques on a scale never witnessed. As straight rows of wheat and barley stretched toward the horizon, Sumerians labored for over three millennia to perfect writing, pottery, economy, administration, education, ranching, and food storage. Canals not very different from those in use on farms today ran across fields overseen by ziggurats: fertile fields planted by lunar calendar and marked by the imprint of an early wheel. Mythology and literature stirred, overseen by the early hero King Gilgamesh, a kind of Sumerian Hercules. Most people lived in the cities.

At first the goddess Inanna, the Sumerian Athena, ruled the capital city of Uruk; but by 2,500 BC, the mountain god Enlil had taken control, watching over a state in which slaves were now captured in battle. (A stormy father, Enlil had tried to kill off humanity by sending down a great a flood.) In 2,400 BC the moon goddess Ningal was said to have abandoned the war-torn city of Ur: like warfare and religion, patriarchy rises with centralized power and expands in lockstep with it, if only because armies need chiefs and troops trained into hyper-macho roles. Such trainable men were willing, then as now, to abandon their families to wage wars of state. Colonization corps radiated outward, eager and determined to harness human, animal, and plant energy to the task of extending a hungry empire.

Around 1,800 BC, expansion came to a halt. By then, the time of Marduk, legendary builder of Babylon, slayer of the generative sea goddess Tiamat, and wielder of the spear named Security and Obedience, many of the cities of Sumer lay deserted, her once-green fields crusted over and ruined. What caused the downfall of the world's first empire?

Among the many firsts of Sumerian civilization, irrigation allowed vast tracts of otherwise dry land to support monocrop agriculture. Unlike horticulture and small-scale farming, how-ever, intensive monocropping eventually brings soil salts to the surface. With no way to lower this salinity, the farmers of Sumer watched crops die and once-rich cropland turn deathly white as Sumerian leaders remained focused on booty, power, and warfare, unaware or uncaring of their dependency on the bounty of nature. What could the farmers do?

Those who did not go under left, as would their kin in Imperial Rome when mining struck down into groundwater and flooded the silver mines that funded the Empire. In fact, the results are always the same wherever empire psycholo-gy—a psychology of hubris, decadence, corruption, violence, and control—represses imaginative ecological sensibilities relied upon by smaller communities to stay in balance with powerful natural forces.

Empires are inherently unsustainable and eventually self-destruct.

3 - Confucius:
Noble Virtues, Rigid Systems

Master Kong (as he was known before his name was Latinized) was born in 551 BC in Qufu in the Chinese state of Lu. According to legend, he was born in response to a prayer uttered by his parents on a holy hill: a *qiu*, which became his personal name. His father, a local military commander, died when the boy was three. To support his family, he grew up caring for animals, looking after parks, and tending a market. After his mother died, Confucius, married since age nineteen, began a career of itinerant teaching while doing some work for the governor of Lu.

As a well-educated man living at the end of the Zhou Dynasty, a time of bronze, ironwork, farming, warfare, and corruption, Confucius came to ask himself what competent leadership might look like. Rivers were redirected and whole valleys irrigated, but court life and politics remained ethically barren and starkly inhumane.

But the ancient sages possessed truths still relevant: love of order, respect for family and ancestry, the divine Mandate of Heaven by which the gods revealed who was fit to rule. Master Kong encouraged his students to steep themselves in the classics to learn how the great minds of antiquity had thought. For this reason he is sometimes referred to as conservative, but in actuality Confucius sought new applications of old truths such as, "Do not do to others what you would not want done to yourself." "Hold faithfulness and humility as first principles." "Economize." "Humaneness is more important than fire or water."

He looked for government to rule by rites, music, honesty, and good example rather than by fear or force. He cautioned his students to be earnest in their intentions and precise and true in their language. Striving for a balanced life, he alternated disciplined scholarship with poetry, dancing, and playing a Chinese zither.

As Master Kong taught, he served for a time in middle age as Minister of Public Works and in other official capacities. With his ongoing emphasis on humanity, knowledge, and integrity, the wonder is that he ever served in any official position at all. Evidently his good manners and reputation secured the buy-in of the Duke of Lu: a golden opportunity to shape government by training its ruler.

Unfortunately, training the ruler proved insufficient when faced by entrenched and widespread corruption and incompetence. When Master Kong's views offended the nobility, he prudently left Lu to look for other leaders to educate. Finding none, he quietly returned in 484 BC to teach, write, and edit anthologies: if he could not transform society through applied wisdom, at least he could preserve knowledge for the future.

It would be difficult to overestimate the impact on that future made by his life and work. At one time no one entered the employ of Chinese government without passing exams on Confucian thought and promising to uphold Confucian values. Beyond China, Master Kong became widely known as a humanist before there were any. Generations of commentators and readers, thinkers and reformers have drawn from the well of wisdom he left intact.

His attempts at reform invite comparison with St. Francis of Assisi, who fought to keep his Order from being diluted by greedy popes who disapproved of his oath of poverty. So completely did the saint's followers forget what he stood for that a day came when Franciscan brothers stood without shame beside Dominicans in the reek and fire of the Inquisition. After the death of Confucius, his ideas were warped and stereotyped by functionaries determined to reduce government to rigid applications of dry edicts whose core of discerning compassion had long been lost.

Long ago, Aristotle had stated that a system is more than the sum of its parts. From the 1950s onward, Systems Theory emerged from a blend of cybernetics, information theory, control theory, and several other timely technologically tinged developments to demonstrate what is evident in the attempts of every reformer, from civil servants and priests to activists and presidents, to change corrupted institutions already headed down the gray hallways of entropy:

Changing or replacing a few elements, even key ones at the top, seldom exerts deep or lasting change on a broken system.

4 - Gnosis:
Inner Light, Outer Darkness

"Those Who Know," they were called by their taunting opponents: *Gnostics*, bands of self-schooled intellectuals and contemplatives who shared with their students the possibility of direct contact with the Divine. Like William James would a thousand years later, they taught that a rich spiritual life was not to be found through arguments or creeds or external proof, but through carefully cultivated internal experience.

In the first few decades after stories of the death of Jesus began to circulate, various groups and sects formed to study what were reputed to be his teachings. As was the custom then, scribes and spiritual masters formulated their own interpretations as narratives eventually known as gospels, a respected educational genre useful for conveying sacred truths through parables and metaphors. Eventually more than thirty of these gospels would make their way through Palestine and cities as far away as Alexandria. From among these early accounts would surface the four selected centuries later as canonical.

This orthodoxy started early. Although Gnosticism predated it, the Gnostics—small schools of spiritual introverts who studied, thought, and meditated together—found themselves under rhetorical attack for being too liberal in the view of an unusually aggressive and literal-minded Christian sect. These Gnostic heretics, complained Irenaeus of Lyons, allowed women to conduct sacred services and teach. Furthermore, they believed that Jesus had been speaking in wisdom stories rather than literal truths and facts; that Eve was a "Messenger of Light" rather than the original sinner who doomed humankind; that the Resurrection was to be taken as an inner experience and not an outer event; and that believers needed only temporary guidance from Those Who Know, after which the instructed were treated as equals, free to pursue their own spiritual path through a world ruled by evil powers.

The Gnostics laughed at their opponents. Only fools took dogma and hellfire literally, called themselves "fathers" although childless, or believed that a woman came out of a man in some lost Garden.

As they laughed, however, the aggressive sect that now called itself *orthodox* (after words that mean "straight" and "right opinion") set itself to accumulate power. Claiming to receive its authority directly from the Apostle Peter, this sect fashioned a papacy in 67 AD from the trappings of ancient Etruscan offices such as the Pontifex Maximus and the Curia. Its "fathers" sorted through extant gospels for those emphasizing obedience to the divinity of Jesus and his followers. These would be "the" Gospels for all time. At the Mons Vaticanus, the "Mount of Soothsayers" where magicians had once collected a fee for casting spells, an elaborate basilica would be built, walled and guarded, with money collected from wealthy patrons threatened with eternal damnation.

By the time this sect's version of Christianity received the official approval of the Roman Empire in 325, when bishops ("overseers") under Constantine formulated a loyalty oath called the Nicene Creed, the Gnostics were no longer laughing. The Emperor banned them a year later, and in 367, Athanasius, Bishop of Alexandria, decreed that all unapproved spiritual texts be burned. Precious Gnostic gospels were hidden in jars and buried in the sands, to be found by accident many centuries later at Nag Hammadi, Egypt and in other fortuitous places.

These writings give us glimpses of the spiritual heights reached by the inner work of Those Who Know, but they also underline the Gnostic distaste for partaking of worldly activity. Like psychotherapists who see therapy as a substitute for activism and political alertness, like everyone who uses contemplation and ritual to hide from the perennial obligation to make a just world, the Gnostic withdrawal of energy from their surroundings only cleared the stage of human affairs for less evolved men to take control of it: men adept at using otherworldly justifications for collecting power and wealth in this world.

The Gnostics did not learn until they were persecuted, if then, that inner transformation decoupled from outer merely enables the ambitious to claim every available office while offering a hand up to their like-minded mental kindred.

Inner work separated from outer action hands over the outer world to ambitious "realists" who seize the hard seats of power and authority.

5 - Boudica:
Return of the Repressed

Rome had occupied wild Britain since 43 AD. The reasons for this were more political than strategic: the new Emperor, Claudius, wanted to impress the citizens and senate of Rome with his military prowess.

Claudius should have known that Britain would be no plum for the picking. Julius Caesar had tried and failed to subdue it a hundred years earlier. Two decades after Claudius's General Aulus Plautius had landed his divisions on the mysterious island of blue-painted people, they were still putting up fierce resistance to Roman rule, and by doing so forcing the Roman government to spend fabulous amounts of money on war.

In 61 AD, indigenous resistance gathered around a tall, red-haired widow: Boudica, head of the Iceni tribe from Norfolk. Upon his death her husband had willed part of the territory he ruled to Emperor Nero for its protection. Instead, Nero had the land seized in its entirety. When Boudica complained about this, the Romans flogged and raped her and her daughters. This proved to be a serious mistake.

Rising in revolt, Boudica (whose name was a Celtic word for "victory") set forth in a chariot followed by a furious horde of native Britons. They marched to the colony of Colchester, then to the new town of London, and then to St. Albans, destroying all three with fire, sharp iron, and elaborate displays of brutality. Thousands of Romans died. Those who survived were sacrificed to the battle goddess Andraste. Roman soldiers attempting a defense were driven in all directions.

As frustrated Nero came to the point of withdrawing the Romans from Britain, General Suetonius Paulinus regrouped and met Boudica's huge army in battle. Boudica had proved a capable guerrilla leader, but, unschooled in military strategy and tactics, she allowed the Romans to choose the field of battle: a narrow strip of land forested on both flanks. Overconfident bystanders watched from afar, expecting another British victory.

Just as the vast Persian army had found itself unable to come fully to grips with the concentrated Spartans and Greeks at Thermopylae, so Boudica's forces were funneled into a small front line as they charged down on the Romans. Unable to bring their longer-range weapons to bear, the Britons were cut down by Roman short swords and javelins. The survivors were routed, and allies of the red-haired Icenian taken prisoner.

What happened to Boudica remains uncertain. The Roman historian Tacitus claims that she poisoned herself, possibly to avoid capture and torture. Others say an illness claimed her. Perhaps she died of a broken heart. Nevertheless, the example she set was not forgotten. Native resistance continued until the Romans finally left Britannia.

Boudica's revolt stands as a reminder that the subjugated always fight back. The human spirit can stand only so much humiliation and powerlessness before it finally rebels. Whether enslaved, enchained, confined behind high walls, hemmed in by colonizers, bankrupted by debtors, or clamped down on by its own internalized persecutor, the repressed always makes a return. When that happens, heaven help the repressors, for by then it will be too late to call 911.

Long-term repression only strengthens the repressed, for as Martin Luther King Jr. observed, "A riot is the language of the unheard."

6 - Nicaea:
Theocracy Divides

In 325, in the lakeside city of Nicaea (now Iznik) in northwestern Turkey, three hundred self-styled bishops met to decide the future of Christendom.

Over three centuries, the dozens of sects that had gathered to study the teachings of Jesus in Palestine, Alexandria, and other sites of learning in the Middle East had been absorbed by or thrust aside by an extremist sect claiming to have inherited the spiritual mantle of St. Peter. Donning the costumes and habits of ancient Etruscan warrior-priests, this band positioned itself on a political platform that denied positions of power to women, confined sacred texts to a male priesthood, encouraged self-sacrifice even to the extreme of death, and upheld the virtues of unquestioning obedience to authority.

On the face of it, their problem with Arius, a teacher and priest from Alexandria, was his belief that Jesus had been born.

One would think this obvious, but the catch for them was what Arius deduced from this: that by making Jesus equal to God, Christians were in fact worshiping two Gods.

Having welded cross to sword by making Christianity the official religion of Rome, the Emperor Constantine agreed to oversee a Council at Nicaea to decide this and other matters of doctrine. Representatives one and all claimed to speak on behalf of the Almighty's concern for heaven-bound sinners.

A learned and eloquent man, Arius made his case—and was shouted down, slapped in the face, stripped of office, excommunicated, and exiled to Palestine for his troubles. Trinitarianism (one God of three Persons) won the day, as did a body of beliefs to be enforced throughout Christendom. The Nicene Creed was made the official pledge. Easter was set for the first Sunday following the full moon after the spring equinox, Constantine having already decided that Christmas would fall on December 25th, a day sacred to the pagan gods Mithras and Saturn. Twenty new canons were put in place. The writings of the Arians were ordered destroyed.

The appearance of unity was consolidated, but as with any rigid facade, it only stimulated the forces of schism at work in the background. Arianism continued, as did other free-thinking "heresies." The bishop of Rome was granted authority over the western Empire, and the bishop of Alexandra authority over the eastern half, setting the stage for further division.

Within five years, Christian missionaries will fan out through Africa to convert supposed savages. His capitol having moved to "Constantinople," Constantine will order his son and wife executed for disloyalty; but by the time he dies, his three other Christian sons will fight over what remains of his Empire. Constantine II, an Arian, ends up in charge of it.

Christian Visigoths will eventually sack Rome, ending the Western Empire. The monk Pelagius will be condemned for proclaiming the original innocence of children, the evils of wealth, and the natural freedom of the soul. Mary, wife of Joseph, is declared a virgin, and Mary Magdalene, companion of Jesus, a whore. Parishioners of Cyril, the Archbishop of Alexandria, burn down the great Library at Alexandria. And on the madness will run, inflaming schism, motivating fights about the true essence of Jesus, setting believers against each other, paying fanatics to go Crusading, exploding into Reformation and Counter-Reformation, forcing Jews to wear badges and live in ghettos (papal order of 1555), propelling Inquisition at the hands of "Holy Comforters," signing the infamous Reich Concordat with Hitler, and all the rest of the long, lamentable, and disastrous record of institutionalized religious power ever vying for total control.

Nor will theocratic madness confine itself to Christendom, not with Zoroastrians battling Muslims, Muslims battling Hindus, Hindus battling Sikhs; not with generations of violence between Israelis and Palestinians; not with supposedly peaceful Buddhists at war in China, Japan, Korea, Mongolia, Tibet, Thailand, Sri Lanka, and India....

When Christian missionaries penetrated new lands, one of their most frequent observations about the aboriginal people they found there was that "they had no religion." True enough. Instead of religion, they enjoyed the kind of nature-friendly spirituality that allowed people in relatively small groups to live with each other in a sacred world. Only with the systematic separation of earth from heaven, lower from higher, man from woman, and self from world does spirituality degenerate into the familiar religious obsession with dogma, authority, power, and control.

History insists on it despite every brief exception to the bloodstained rule:

An absolutist emphasis on an invisible heaven paves the way for hellish results to disorder this world.

7 - Temujin:
Revenge of the Tortured Child

When Temujin was born in 1162, the people of Mongolia were divided into clans so violent that survival into old age constituted something of a miracle. War chiefs rode at the head of hordes of scimitar-wielding cavalry, terrorizing as often as they governed. Clubs, pikes, and blades paid off old grievances while tearing open fresh ones. Blood feuds wiped out entire families. Slow torture was a commonplace, a sadistic sport for the powerful.

At the age of nine, Temujin learned that his father, the head of a local clan, had been poisoned by a rival. Eager for new leadership, the clan cast the boy and his mother and sister out into the cold.

Forced to live in poverty, they struggled for twelve years until Temujin was captured by a marauding clan and placed in a stock. When a sympathetic witness freed him, the boy escaped and hid until the danger of recapture had passed.

This was by no means the end of his trials. Another clan captured his mother, forcing him to ally with yet another clan to free her by force. He also had to liberate his young wife Börte after she had been imprisoned and raped.

Along the way Temujin had gained powerful allies. When they realized his ambitions rose higher than heading a clan as one more armed bully among many, they brought friends willing to be trained in his unusual fighting tactics. Temujin, they saw, worked not just to lead another horde into battle: he was forging a disciplined weapon the like of which Mongolia had never seen. For what purpose? His self-appointed task was to politically unify this great mass of land, something no one had ever accomplished. A land in which children could grow up safely.

As he conquered his rivals and added their troops to his own, his appreciative men gave him a new title: Genghis Khan (Great Khan).

The force he led was not a horde, but neither did it move like a stand-up army. Faced with superior numbers, his men had learned to melt away, dispersing into the countryside to form up again later, this time behind their opponents. Or they would ride in feigned retreat, leading their attackers into a well-planned ambush. The least of them could accurately hit a moving target with an arrow while riding at a full gallop. Centuries before the Pony Express, relay riders provided their khan with up-to-date information on distant realms. His intelligence service delivered such accurate information that he often knew more about enemy troop movements than their own generals did.

Part of his success rested on the battle-hardened shoulders of the able men he picked as commanders. Temujin understood how to earn loyalty, how to delegate, and how to reward victory. After his death, one of his generals, Sabutai, almost conquered Hungary, a move that would have left Europe open to Mongolian invasion.

For centuries the West has viewed Temujin as a villain, but many in Mongolia still see him as a kind of King Arthur, a bringer of order and unity. The legal code he enforced to end centuries of wanton butchery was the first of its kind in that region of the world, there at the heart of an empire of plains and steppes, its immensity reaching across nearly all of Asia. It is said that when some former enemies brought him their dead khan as a gesture of surrender and good faith, he ordered them executed. When they asked why, the response must have shocked everyone in earshot, never having heard its like: "You broke the law."

Eventually Temujin's empire went the way of all empires, force never having been an adequate substitute for cultural evolution; but the impressions it left lasted long after his death, as did one of its crucial lessons:

Any culture that allows the mistreatment of children sets itself up to be conquered by them.

8 - Tenochtitlan:
Catastrophic Denial

When sailing vessels under Hernando Cortes had passed over the Gulf of Mexico to land at what is now Veracruz ("True Cross") in 1519, Moctezuma, chief of the Aztecs, dispatched gift-bearing emissaries to greet the newcomers: armored men who promptly fired off a cannon to intimidate their feather-garbed greeters.

When the newcomers then showed up at the Aztec capital city of Tenochtitlan uninvited—in fact the Emperor had asked them not to come at all—more gifts were dispensed, this time of gold and precious gems, in the belief that the odd, pale soldiers could be appeased. *We Spanish suffer from a strange disease of the heart,* explained Cortes with psychopathic cynicism, *for which the only known remedy is gold.* Like Columbus, he had owned famished slaves who died mining the metal for him in Hispanola and in Cuba.

31

The Spaniards showed their gratitude for their gifts, their fine guest homes, their seats of honor, and their food, drink, and Aztec hospitality by defacing their hosts' sacred imagery, referring to them as "heathens," ordering them around, and causing fear with displays of unsheathed weaponry. Still the Aztecs held their temper, convinced that courtesy and generosity would win over these barbaric conquistadors.

While Cortes was away, rumors spread of a secretly planned Aztec uprising. To show these cunning heathens he meant business, Alvarado, second in command, caught several hundred members of the Aztec ruling class feasting one night, closed the doors behind him, and murdered them in cold blood.

If there had been no planned revolt before, one certainly flared up now as furious warriors chased the band of conquistadors from Tenochtitlan, shedding bullets and dropped treasures on their hasty way out.

Resuming command when he returned, Cortes lay siege to the city, cutting its fresh water supply and killing Aztecs who emerged to gather food. That they were civilians did not matter to their murderers at all. "It was perfect slaughter," Cortes bragged in a letter to King Charles of Spain.

It is impossible to know how many Aztecs and other New World natives fell during and after Tenochtitlan. Estimates run as high as ninety million, some done away with by European diseases like syphilis. Moctezuma perished while in the Spaniards' custody and vanished from history. Cortes lived on in statues, parks, and avenues named after him.

The Aztec rulers, and for that matter the citizens, had every reason to believe their guests to be professional killers whose only interest was in stealing as much booty as possible. Yet they managed to convince themselves that all would turn out for the best. Nor is this habit found only among the People of the Fifth Sun now set forever. Again and again, individuals, families, neighborhoods, whole nations turn away from facing the unpleasant reality of danger at the doorstep. According to

Lewis Mumford, when armed invaders came to overthrow the Roman city of Hippo as the Empire fell, the first sound they heard was a roaring from the circus of spectators more concerned about their dose of entertainment than about their own survival. Holocaust survivor Elie Wiesel tells a tragic story of a woman in his village who dreamed of flames and tried to call a warning. Nobody believed her, and the entire village was hauled away in cattle cars to face the ovens of Auschwitz.

Denial kills.

9 - Bartolome:
A Man Not Of His Time

By the time Isabella I of Castile married Ferdinand II of Aragon in 1469, the year Niccolo Machiavelli was born, centuries of cultural advancement in Spain stood on the verge of being undone. As power passed from the Islamic Moors to the Christians under Ferdinand and Isabella, secret police and Inquisitors waited in the wings.

Empire-building requires money, however. Stories of fabulous Far Eastern wealth had been circulating through Europe since Marco Polo returned from China, but the Muslims (who had seized Constantinople) controlled many of the key land routes eastward. The sea stood open, however, so the Spanish Crown paid Genoan navigator Christopher Columbus, the first of a series of conqueror-explorers, to find and bring back gold.

Bound for Asia, Columbus ran into Hispanola instead and proceeded to enslave some of its native people: Arawaks (or

Tainos) who would find themselves all but extinguished one day soon on plantations set up by the Admiral of the Ocean Sea. This set a bloody precedent continued by Cortes and other ambitious men determined to plunder the New World while funding colonization through the slave trade.

One of these adventurers brought back a slave to Seville to give his young son Bartolome, who at age nine had seen some of Columbus's wretched captives paraded through the streets. In 1502, father and son sailed to Hispanola (the future Haiti and Dominican Republic) to cash in on the burgeoning trade in human life and labor.

Although well-educated by the church, Las Casas the younger, a priest in training, felt no qualms at first about managing a manor staffed by native slaves. He also did not object to accompanying Governor Ovando's murderous pacification expeditions. As Adolf Eichmann would claim centuries later at Nuremberg, Las Casas was following orders. Nevertheless, the suffering and bloodshed he saw began to work on him. The Arawaks were routinely starved, maimed, tortured, and mutilated by religious men who did not consider them human. The native population began to decline.

In December of 1511, Dominican friar Antonio Montesino gave a speech denouncing the New World slave system as evil. After being denounced by Columbus's son Diego and other conquistadors who benefited from this system, Montesino was shipped back to Spain, but not before Las Casas had heard his denunciation. This too did its silent work.

On Pentecost in 1514, Las Casas freed his slaves and publicly added his voice to Montesino's. This convinced the king of Spain and Cardinal Ximenes de Cisneros to look into the matter. While they did, Las Casas continued to preach against the abuse of native peoples while compiling written documentation on their behalf. He also experimented successfully (after an episode of failure caused by forces beyond his control) with peaceful, respectful contact with natives of South America, after which he turned his tireless attention to defending the rights of enslaved black Africans. Upon returning to Spain, he set free slaves still being held in Seville.

As a result of these years of struggle, years that included death threats and accusations of treason, a series of church laws and a papal bull finally agreed that native people were human beings fully deserving of basic rights. An attempt to deprive the Inca of whatever treasures remained to them fell through partly because of Las Casas, still fighting for indigenous rights at the age of eighty-two. He died that year in a convent in Madrid.

When the unsavory side of some idealized public figure comes under scrutiny, the excuse is often raised that "he was a man of his time." Christopher Columbus, for instance: a "man of his time" who told the Crown to use the Arawaks as slave labor because they were fit, generous, easy to order around, eager to please, and in possession of gold. John Mason, who sold Pequot survivors into slavery after killing several hundred at Mystic River: a "man of his time." Thomas Jefferson: a "man of his time" for having sex with his female slaves.

In some ways Las Casas too remained a man of his time. He watched many years of brutality before finally liberating his slaves. He remained a member of the church that gave religious comfort and abundant rationalization for what red-handed conquistadors perpetrated throughout the New World. Before turning against African slavery, he recommended it as an alternative to overworking the vanishing Arawaks. He continued to believe that missionary work could prove benevolent if peacefully conducted despite its clearly disastrous colonial record.

Yet he rose above his time by aspiring to a higher ethical standard than that of other men around him, some of whom had been his mentors. Their disagreement pained him personally and threatened him professionally. In spite of this he fought for the right of indigenous people to govern themselves on their own land. He did this because he came to understand that true cultural and spiritual evolution comes about through dissent, never through blind compliance.

Every age, and every place, contains people like Las Casas, and their actions in the service of integrity and humanity necessitate a challenging but inspiring realization:

No matter what social pressures are brought to bear, we all retain the capacity to rise above our time when higher obligations demand it.

10 - Nagashino:
A Failure to Adapt

It is June of 1575 in Mikawa Province on the southern coast of Japan. Okudaira Sadamasa, a feudal lord, commands a force of samurai defending a castle squatting in a broad plain at Nagashino. The castle looks ominously down on the vulnerable supply lines of Takeda Katsuyori, chief of the Takedas. He is furious at Okudaira's betrayal of loyalty and means to make him pay for it by unleashing a force of 15,000 against him.

Coming to Okudaira's defense are two fabled commanders: Oda Nobunaga, uniter of the Oda clan, a seasoned warlord famous for his numerous conquests, and Tokagawa Ieyasu, future shogun (by 1600) and model for novelist James Clavell's famous schemer Lord Toranaga. Among their men wait 1,000 samurai loading their firearms.

Takeda knows about the firearms, and he is not impressed: the rain will make them difficult to fire. Besides, he has beaten Oda and Tokagawa before. And he too wields a potent weapon: a burly, seasoned wing of expert cavalry.

At his signal, samurai on horseback sweep down on the combined force of their opponents, pausing only to ford a small stream. To their dismay they find a series of wooden barricades erected to nullify the impact of men on horseback. They charge anyway.

When they do, they meet a second surprise: staggered volley fire unleashed by Oda's gunners. The gunners stand in three ranks, with at least one rank firing while the others reloaded.

Under this more or less continual concentration of bullets the Takeda force withered; by afternoon it was forced to retreat, most of its generals dead in the mud, as a second Oda army relieved the castle. (Impressed by Okudaira's stolid defense of it, Oda gave it to him and allowed him to change his name from Sadamasa to Nobumasa.)

Firearms had been used in battle before, but never with such deadly effect. From that point onward, their role would come to dominate field warfare. The age of chivalry was coming to an end in Japan, just as in Europe when the English longbow and its armor-piercing arrows had caught King John of France flat-footed at the Battles of Crécy (1346) and Poitiers (1356).

To the victor belongs the fruits of innovation. Marshal Maurice de Saxe relied on artillery, as ever general of his time did, but he fired it obliquely to maximize its scattering effect against massed blocks of troops. At Cynoscephalae (197 BC), the omni-directional Roman legion put a definitive end to the forward-pointing Macedonian phalanx.

These examples of the superiority of innovation are military, but others could easily be found: solid state circuitry trumping Swiss chronometry; family gardens in Cuba replacing monocrop agriculture deprived of petroleum by American embargo; electronic communications surpassing those of paper; small-group "collaborative inquiry" wisdom solving problems more effectively than the "lone genius" approach...

Old methods might be difficult to surrender, especially when steeped in hoary ideologies, but in the end, the strict imperative governing nature's relentless evolutionary experimentation exerts its fateful hold everywhere:

Adapt or die.

11- Plague:
Unsanctioned Ways of Knowing

In 1665, the Black Death visited London.

It was called "Black Death" because of the darkening lumps it left on the infected. The original plague had reduced the population of Western Europe. At the height of this plague, which broke out one April in the dockyards and was ignored by the authorities until the upper classes caught it, 7,000 people a day were swept out of existence as lords, merchants, and clergy fled the city. Guards were posted to keep victims in their homes.

Fires that supposedly cleansed the air of disease and evil spirits burned all day and night, giving the city a ghastly, hellish glow. Ironically, a great fire would break out in London a year later. It was as though the Christian underworld had found its place topside. Believers lashed themselves with whips, blaming themselves for it and make it go away.

43

As panic spread, a few level-headed people noticed the presence of rats in infected neighborhoods. What if the rats had something to do with the plague? Making their intuitive musings known, these inquirers were met with derision by scientists who argued that such a wild claim had no proof behind it. In a sense the scientists were right: Robert Koch would not be around to prove the existence of germs until 1890.

Instead, the Lord Mayor of London ordered all dogs and cats destroyed in the hope this would contain the spread of disease. In hindsight this probably made the plague stronger by removing animals who ate the rats.

When the reaping finally ended, at least 20% of London's 500,000 residents were dead.

History provides many examples of intuitive warnings ignored for want of "proof" or quantifiable evidence: last-minute pleas to stay off the *Titanic*, spiritualists moving their tribe uphill just before a tsunami rolls in, Caesar's wife begging him not to go meet with the Senate on the day of his assassination. When James Dean showed off his fancy new sports car to Sir Alec Guinness, the older actor turned to him and grimly predicted that Dean would die in it. A few weeks later Guinness heard the news and was horrified. He had had no proof. But he knew.

When the speculation bubble burst and the world economy began to melt down in 2008, it did so after months, even years, of warnings by seasoned financial planners ignored by number crunchers and computer modelers who thought they knew better. After all, they held master's degrees in business, they were recognized experts, and they relied on solid calculations and state-of-the-art equipment.

They were wrong, and millions of people plunged into poverty and homelessness because of it.

Scientific knowledge provides welcome verification but has never been humanity's sole means of knowing.

12 - Salem:
Self-Hatred Turned Outward

"Let us get this straight. We allow you citizenship as equals, without requiring onerous paperwork. We educate your family. We do not persecute you for beliefs, as was done to you in England. Nevertheless, you are leaving because you want an old book to rule your lives, and you think our 'liberalism' is poisoning the minds of your children. You plan to board a leaky vessel and sail across the Atlantic to a land you've never seen. And you think this land is a Terrestrial Paradise. What can we say? Bon voyage."

Probably no such conversation took place in Leyden, Holland, in 1620, but if it had, it would not have wandered far from the truth of the matter. After returning to England long enough to charter their vessel, the small group of dissident Christians sailed for Virginia but made landfall instead in Massachusetts. History books call them "Pilgrims." In two decades, thousands would enter New England.

The Pilgrims were Puritans—reformers calling for a "purification" of worship—of the Separatist type who could not live with the Church of England and yearned to be elsewhere. Ever on guard against temptations of the flesh, they lived simply and without ornamentation. Even their churches were bare, stripped of all possible "idolatrous" imagery. Only the decorative steeple was permitted because it pointed skyward at a benevolent but vengeful God.

Illnesses, crop failures, and inclement weather were signs of His displeasure. By 1689, the year preacher Cotton Mather's *Memorable Providences Relating to Witchcrafts and Possessions* heightened fear throughout New England, all public and many private affairs were governed theocratically, and by men only, with the Bible held up as supreme authority.

In January of 1692, Betty Parris and Abigail Williams, daughter and niece of minister Samuel Parris, began to act strangely, having fits as though possessed. Soon other Salem Village girls were "possessed," including Elizabeth Hubbard and Ann Putnam. Under intense social pressure, three of the supposedly afflicted girls identified three women as the source of their fits: Sarah Osborne, who seldom went to church, Sarah Good, who was poor, and Tituba, a slave of Reverend Parris. They were arrested, interrogated, and jailed.

Of the dozens of women soon to be tried for the capital crime of witchcraft, many were single, widowed, or owners of land. Martha Corey was arrested for publicly questioning the accuracy of the accusations, and Sarah Cloyce for defending her accused sister. Four-year-old Dorothy Good was forced to testify against her own mother. Desperate confessions wrung from women frightened at the prospect of hanging amplified the confusion.

By May, a special court was busy trying "witches" in Essex, Middlesex, and Suffolk Counties. Sarah Osborne became the first suspect to die in jail. In June, Bridget Bishop was the first to be hanged. All in all, a hundred and fifty were arrested and jailed, six died in jail, twenty-nine were convicted, and nineteen—fourteen women and five men—were hanged. Giles Corey refused to enter a plea and died with heavy stones piled on his chest. Tituba was sold.

With the force of rage and paranoia now spent on scapegoats, the questioning belatedly began. Captain John Alden was cleared, as were others brought before grand juries. In Salem Village, where Ann Putnam applied for church membership in 1706, she claimed to have been deluded by the devil into making false accusations. The church that had cast the accused from its doors welcomed their accuser.

Why did this catastrophe happen at the hands of people who thought of themselves as "the godly"? Explanations range from Salem citizens' dislike of their new Reverend Parris (did his daughter act out in response to it?) to tainted groundwater. Certainly it's no accident that the first of the accused was a woman of color, and that most of those hanged were women.

It would be naïve to lay all the blame on Puritan Separatist beliefs: humans as inherently evil, the world as a dark hell of misery, women as stained by the sin of Eve, the flesh as a source of corruption. People hold such beliefs as befit their psychology, and the psychology always comes first. Those who see human nature as basically trustworthy under optimal conditions will create a different society than those who see it as evil and in need of breaking and harsh control.

The naturally growthful impulses of human nature seek to experience themselves as an integrated whole. They cannot be thwarted without serious internal and social consequences. To believe oneself sinful, evil, and deserving of endless misery opens a core shame-based wound of smoldering self-contempt. The rage this engenders must go somewhere.

The miserable soul who self-flagellates with shoulds, oughts, and sadistically rigid standards will eventually apply them to others, with predictable results. It is impossible to treat oneself sadistically without projecting that sadism elsewhere.

At bottom, hatred is as non-selective as lava. (Conversely, long-standing hatred of others diminishes oneself.)

When belief in non-worth is shared, when inhumane judgmentalism is internalized and enshrined, the group which institutionalizes it must have scapegoats upon whom to periodically release the long-pent rage that always results from outer oppression internalized. A rage that, like hellfire, never blows out.

Sooner or later, chronic self-hatred enlarges into hatred of humanity, of scapegoats, and ultimately of the world.

13 - Wovoka:
Tradition Versus Regression

By 1889, a year of fierce, killing blizzards raging across the United States, most Native Americans had been confined to reservations. Those who survived this imprisonment suffered from cold and hunger; the lands to which they had been forcibly moved were for the most part infertile, and promised supplies of rations and clothing often never arrived. As Native children were placed in schools that forbid them the use of their own language, missionaries showed up on the reservations in search of potential converts.

1889 was also the year that a Northern Paiute medicine man named Wovoka claimed to find inspiration in a dream during the solar eclipse. He dreamed, he reported from Nevada, that all the white conquerors would disappear very soon into the earth, leaving it for the Indians to enjoy. The sacred buffalo and other slain animal beings would return in happiness, the shades of the ancestors would return as well, and the Indians would be free of the sorrow of conquest—but only if they went back to ceremonial cleansings, communal chantings, traditional crafts, and prayer. They also had to do a special dance.

The dance was to last for five grueling days and was to be performed every six weeks, followed each time by a ritual bath. Dancers moved in a circle, a common Native American pattern, while asking the spirit world for assistance. Within a year, the dance was spreading out from people who had come to Nevada to hear the words of Wovoka. Hundreds, then thousands participated.

With the dance went word that Jesus was coming to save the people, and that perhaps Wovoka himself was Jesus. This must have sounded strange to families whose children had been taken away by emissaries of the white man's god and taught to hate themselves and their culture. Some of this might have originated with Mormon missionaries who believed that Jesus had visited Native America long ago. Some of it might have reflected the upbringing of Wovoka himself, who in childhood had been taken in by Christian ranchers who renamed him Jack Wilson. It was also said that Wovoka was immune to bullets and could control the weather.

Although what came to be called the Ghost Dance had its roots in other Native movements guided by other visionaries, it brought shattered tribes together as nothing else had been able to do. Prominent Indian leaders like Kicking Bear and Sitting Bull were involved in it.

Of course, all this worried the U.S. Government. Hopeless people can be dominated, but hopeful ones fight back. Never mind that Wovoka spread a message of peaceful non-cooperation, or that religious revivals commonly included dancing: the Ghost Dance must be banned.

Naturally, this merely made it more popular (see Chapter 5) and confirmed to the dancers that they were on the right track: if the conquering whites opposed it so vehemently, then it must be good and worth doing.

Finally, the order went out from the Bureau of Indian Affairs to arrest Sitting Bull, a Lakota Sioux leader, even though he had never taken the Dance very seriously. In the resulting melee, Sitting Bull and a number of enforcement agents were killed. In response, the Seventh Cavalry rode forth to pacify the Sioux, one result of which was the 1890 massacre of Sioux civilians by rifle and machine gun fire at Wounded Knee Creek. No messiah arrived to save them.

Going back to the "old ways" is a common human response to oppression and cultural downfall. When the Christianized Roman Empire crumbled, a brief revival of pagan polytheism flickered and then went out. In our time, when numerous "back to nature" programs offer attractive packages for staging a return to Eden, the malcontented seize upon symbols and ceremonies appropriated from Native American and other cultures in order to summon forth a golden agrarian past. But symbols and ceremonies are not magic wands, and retreats from the present cannot constitute a viable future.

The disaster is not that people respect their traditions, resist assimilation, and preserve the lore that keeps their culture alive. The disaster is when the "old ways" are literalized, romanticized, and dogmatized instead of renewed and reinterpreted for changing times. Even warrior-shaman Black Elk believed that Ghost Shirts made during the Dance would deflect bullets....until he saw the horror of Wounded Knee.

In the long run, perhaps Wovoka's vision was correct, and the final joke will be on those who disrespect the Earth. They are bound to go under, for as Gary Snyder pointed out, "Nature bats last." For now, however, we are faced with another lesson:

Clinging conservatively to traditional procedures, rites, and rituals instead of renewing them hastens cultural decline.

14 - Paris:
The Self-Spinning Cycle of Violence

When the French monarchy and its bankers had drained dry the middle class and squandered the people's money to the point of making them poor, they revolted, their anger all the hotter from pretend reforms that reformed nothing. Having tried unsuccessfully to tax the wealthy nobility, Louis XVI and Marie Antoinette were arrested and guillotined.

Rather than being silenced or healed, polarizations only widened. The Revolutionary Tribunal and the Committee of Public Safety swung into action on behalf of the revolutionary government, a National Convention that was busy warring on England and Holland even while making lists of potentially disloyal French citizens. As huge amounts of money were diverted into national defense, foreigners and moderates suspected of disagreement with new government policy were put under surveillance. Juries tried and convicted on the basis of hearsay. Hungry hordes joined the French army as conscripts, swelling its ranks.

From September 1793 to July 1794, thousands of heads rolled in Paris alone. Under flapping flags, patriotic axemen wheeled guillotines out into the countryside in search of more "traitors." Thomas Paine was jailed. Officials spread terror in the name of combatting terrorism. The supposed triumph of reason over superstition had lost its head.

This provoked a counter-reaction.

Maximilien de Robespierre, an attorney seated on both the Convention and the Committee, had conveniently put away his former thoughts about peace and human rights when he saw where the crimson wind was blowing. After having his opponents executed, he went even farther and, as president of the Convention, instituted laws that allowed indictments without judges, juries, or witnesses (see Chapter 25). Accusation by the president was now enough to end a French life, in France or on foreign soil.

Realizing that he could legally try anyone, the deputies revolted, and in 1794, Robespierre and twenty-one of his supporters met the National Razor. More followed in the "White Terror," a violent reaction to the Reign of Terror. Persecuted former moderates now controlled the levers of retribution.

In a year the Convention was replaced with the Directory, a republican body created by the new constitution. But few trusted it, especially after its rigging of elections, ongoing purges, obvious corruption, and contempt for the constitution whose laws it suspended at will in the name of national security. Enough former revolutionaries injured by the White Terror remained to organize armed resistance: a counter-counter-reaction revolving on the endless wheel of violence.

Once again the army was called out, this time to protect the failing Directory. One of the generals who helped quell the uprisings was made supreme commander of all French forces. It was thought a popular hero would appeal to the people, and for a time, he did. His name was Napoleon Bonaparte.

Whatever flashpoints we examine—India, Ireland, the Middle East, China, anywhere—the bitter story is always the same:

Violence always ignites more violence.

15 - Freud:
Taboo Totemism

Not long after Pierre Janet began experimenting in France with what he called "psychological analysis," a new set of techniques for uncovering and healing unconscious trauma, Freud expanded the "cathartic method" supposedly developed by his colleague Josef Breuer into a new treatment approach called "psychoanalysis." "Supposedly" because Breuer had never done any cathartic work beyond listening patiently to patients' stories and applying occasional hypnosis.

Underdogs ever attract malcontents. Soon a small study circle of physicians and intellectuals gathered around Freud, the Vienna medical establishment's latest rogue practitioner, to study the new approach. These men recognized, as Freud did, that psychoanalysis opened up possibilities of cultural analysis far beyond the consulting room.

These Wednesday night meetings normally consisted of

papers read and critiqued as heated debate and cigar smoke thickened the air. Acrimony developed early as participants shifted their attacks from the points under discussion to the person defending them. Commenting on this *ad hominem* habit openly was likely to elicit accusations of "resistance" or of not having analyzed oneself enough. (At Salem, women defending themselves vigorously against charges of being in league with Satan were often considered exemplary examples of the Evil One's power to deceive the unaware.)

Firmly entrenched in the mechanistic worldview dominant since the Scientific Revolution, Freud and his followers regarded the psyche as an intricate machine actuated by pathways and conduits of erotic energy. All "higher" aspirations like kindness, creativity, compassion, and spirituality were to be suspected as self-deceptions raised to conceal the nature of the machinery. Sex and death were the two primal programs that operated the psyche. Everything else in human life derived from these two drives.

Although the members of the Psychological Wednesday Society were atheists, the language they used soon began to show signs of a religious charge. Psychoanalysis was "the cause." Those who disagreed with its precepts were "dissidents" or, in the case of Adler and Jung, who left the Freudian circle of brothers, "heretics." When those who questioned were suspected of being "disloyal" to "the Professor," Ernest Jones formed a secret inner circle called The Committee. Members received a signet ring to seal their support of Freud, who, flattered by all this, compared himself to Charlemagne being protected by knightly paladins.

The question has been raised of how a "movement" so rich in ambition but poor in actual curative power survived. The relatively few early cures remained dubiously documented or, as in the case of Anna O, diagnosed with hysteria and seen by Breuer, were patently false. In fact, patients like Viktor Tausk and Pauline Silberstein, former patients like Eugenia Sokolnicka and Mabbie Burlingham, and analysts like

Wilhelm Stekel, Herbert Silberer, and Paul Federn killed themselves. After publishing a fradulent *Diary of an Adolescent Girl*, Hermine Hug-Helmuth was murdered by her nephew Rudolph, who testified that her relentless analysis of him had driven him mad.

Several analysts had affairs with patients: Harry Stack Sullivan with Jimmy Inscoe (age fifteen), Sandor Ferenczi with Gizella Palos and her daughter, Carl Jung with Maria Moltzer, Toni Wolff, and Sabina Spielrein, cocaine addict Otto Gross with most of his female patients.... Ernest Jones was accused of molesting children and left his country because of it. Otto Rank began every analysis by telling all his patients that they suffered from "birth trauma." Ferenczi asked his patients to analyze *him*, and Karl Abraham ignored the obvious battle anguish of German combat veterans while focusing on their toilet training. Not above arranging lives and marriages of patients to secure large donations, Freud worried for years at a dream in which he injected a female patient with poison.

Destructive incompetence continued into the next generation, with Karen Horney sleeping with her supervisees, George Zilboorg misdiagnosing the brain tumor that killed Gershwin, and Melanie Klein writing up her children as clinical cases. Her real cases still astound the reader: how could anyone emotionally incest children so thoroughly by projecting her own perverse fantasies onto them—and get away with it?

Scholars have suggested that World War I helped keep psychoanalysis alive by supporting its emphasis on the depths of human destructiveness. If anything, the war delayed matters by keeping analysts from meeting and promoting their work at international conferences.

What's important to bear in mind is that the followers of psychoanalysis believed they were promoting an intellectual and cultural crusade, with Freud their prophet and chief "conquistador" (his term). The movement decked itself out in the trappings of a secular religion: a special vocabulary for those in the know, a circle of priests, the confessional consulting room, the analyzed as initiants, a ruling trinity (id, ego, super-ego), battles over doctrine, founding scriptures, and even a theory of redemption: "where there was id [unconsciousness], there shall ego [consciousness] be." Psychoanalysis offered an unconscious religious system to intellectuals for whom Yahweh and Jesus no longer served. Not for nothing did Hanns Sachs compare training analyses to religious initiations. (This lends a tint of irony to the fate of Karl Abraham, who swallowed a fish bone and died on Christmas.)

The alchemists once advised inspecting the manure for the gold within it. Freud and his pioneers, however neurotic, did leave bits of gold to be worked with. As a result, contemporary psychoanalysis has moved far behind its shadowy beginnings. Analysts now work with field theory, group supervision, neurobiology, and practical theories of unconscious interaction far more complex than linear models of who projects what into whom. Some practitioners even describe the self as a *story* animated by recurring, self-structuring motifs. The name of the apostate Jung has been spotted in psychoanalytic journals.

Still, the tinge and aura of ritualism remain as cautionary reminder and historical lesson:

Scratch a materialist and find a believer with a doctrine, from the libidinous hydraulics of Freudianism to the all-creating monotheism of the "selfish gene."

Systems and theories that shrink human nature to its material components eventually take on the trappings of unconscious evangelism.

16 - Rockefeller:
Pipelines of Darkness

Every year the U.S. Government subsides the petroleum industry with $17.18 billion in tax breaks and $1.7 billion in grants, programs, and research. Those amounts do not include $6 billion a month in Iraq, $12 billion a month in Afghanistan (with its access to the oil and gas resources of the Caspian Sea), covert actions against Iran or Venezuela, or $55-96.3 billion annually allocated by the U.S. Department of Defense for guarding petroleum supplies around the world. Two-thirds of those supplies flow from the Persian Gulf. (Oil company encroachments on Arab territory are why the Arabs stopped fighting each other and gathered under common cause.)

The petroleum lobby is one of the three largest in Washington. Backed by the U.S. Chamber of Commerce, giant oil companies funnel $500,000 *per minute* to terrorism-sponsoring nations in which rape victims are flogged for getting pregnant and women cannot drive at all and cannot walk the streets without a male escort.

All the major oil companies spend generously on political campaigns, with 70% going to Republicans. In the case of George W. Bush in 2000, that included $34 million. Exxon was the top spender. Banks are heavily involved in oil too, especially Goldman Sachs, Citi, JP Morgan, Chase, and Bank of America. Between 1992 and 2005, the World Bank Group spent over $28 billion on fossil fuel projects.

Such an extreme degree of dependency on the dark rivers of fire formerly confined below imposes many additional costs. Road congestion drained from America's top seventy cities $74 billion for 4.6 million lost hours and 6.7 billion wasted gallons of fuel. Over the past twenty years, the world has seen thirty oil spills larger than the *Exxon Valdez*, and daily gasoline runoff from streets and driveways soaks eleven million gallons—one *Exxon Valdez* oil spill—into American waterways every eight months according to the National Academy of Sciences. In fact, the oil and gas industries leave behind more solid and liquid waste than all other municipal, agricultural, mining, and industrial sources combined.

Although refineries pumped over 250 million tons of carbon dioxide into the air in 2004 and constitute the second greatest stationary source of greenhouse gases, Exxon alone employs forty front companies to kill regulatory legislation and to make climate change research findings seem uncertain. Additionally, refineries spew carcinogens and toxins that cause leukemia, lymphatic tissue cancers, birth defects, bronchitis, and emphysema.

Victims of more overt violence include the Huastecs of Veracruz, the Osages and Poncas of Oklahoma, the Ogoni of the Niger Delta, Nigerians of Opia and Ikenyan, the Acehnese of Indonesia, Burmese villagers tortured and enslaved, the Kichwa of Ecuador, the Gwich'in of Alaska, Amazonians ill from toxic waste, and many other native people victimized by genocide, rape, kidnapping, murder, torture, starvation, thirst, pollution, population displacement, gunfire from helicopters, and villages set on fire from above—all of it funded by big petroleum.

It wasn't always like this. All of it and more crawled out into the world from the polished desk of John D. Rockefeller, shadowy father of the multinational corporation and ambitious founder of Big Oil.

In 1863, Rockefeller, son of a salesman father who impersonated a doctor and a devout Baptist mother who beat him to improve him, put down some money for a new oil refinery in Cleveland, Ohio. By 1870, he did so well that he incorporated Standard Oil, with himself as its largest shareholder. Detached, hidden, ghostlike, and spectral, Rockefeller bullied the railroads into giving Standard special rates, then secretly bought out his languishing competitors, turning their owners into spies pretending to still be doing business as independents. Installing pipelines to further reduce the influence of rail, he set up a trust to bypass laws designed to stop corporations from growing too powerful. By 1919, Standard provided 26% of all U.S. oil production, with 70% of Standard's business done overseas away from regulation.

The Sherman Anti-Trust Act had been signed in part to break up the sprawling company nicknamed "Anaconda" and "the Monster," but the Act was feebly enforced. Meanwhile Standard's network of spies, assassins, arsonists, extortionists, and bought politicians and lawyers grew, as did its immense revenues. "To believe that the Standard Oil Combination, or any other similar aggregation, would lower prices except under the pressure of the competition they were trying to kill, argues an amazing gullibility," wrote Ida Tarbell in 1904 in response to suggestions that business could regulate itself. (Incidentally, Tarbell was a descendant of Rebecca Nurse, hung at Salem for witchcraft.) "For centuries the struggle of the nations has been to obtain stable government, with fair play to the masses. To obtain this we have hedged our kings and emperors and presidents about with a thousand constitutional restrictions...And yet we have here in the United States allowed men practically autocratic powers in commerce." Safe behind closed doors, Rockefeller coldly assured his competitors that resistance was futile.

When Standard Oil was finally ordered to disburse, it simply rearranged itself into several new companies, each controlled by Rockefeller and his associates. The largest fragment became Exxon, a meaningless two-syllable name chosen because it sounded impressive. In 2006, Exxon became the most profitable corporation in history, earning $39.5 billion in profits in a single year. The other spinoffs, including Mobile, Chevron, Gulf, and Texaco, were not far behind.

Eventually British Petroleum and Dutch-owned Shell would join the world's dominant petroleum cartel: high-finance pushers controlling the black, poisonous substance to which industrial civilization remains addicted. Drilled landscapes would subside in literal depressions as pipelines sucked forth and injected their slimy liquids like gigantic syringes. Atmosphere and oceans would begin to die. And the oil wars would go on.....

Leaving positions of power unwatched and unregulated makes them vulnerable to capture by unbalanced minds obsessed with control.

17 - Mulholland:
Problem-Growing Engineering

"WE, THE FARMING COMMUNITIES OF OWENS VALLEY, BEING ABOUT TO DIE, SALUTE YOU."

In March of 1927, this notice appeared in the *Los Angeles Times* as a gigantic aqueduct constructed by the Los Angeles Water District under engineer William Mulholland sucked the water out of Owens Lake two hundred and fifty miles to the east in Inyo County. The Water District had once been publicly owned, but it was privatized in 1898. Work on the aqueduct began in 1913 after Los Angeles citizens were frightened into believing they were running out of water.

But the aqueduct did not run to Los Angeles. It landed in the San Fernando Valley on 100,000 acres recently purchased by the same local oligarchs who had called for its construction. An investigative reporter who had written about water being spilled from the city system late at night lost his job.

In order to secure the aqueduct at the Owens Valley end, the oligarchs had bought up 262,102 acres of farmland, thereby putting more than a thousand farmers out of business. When the aqueduct went online, the sole source of irrigation for orchards, grains, alfalfa, and other crops planted and harvested by the people of five towns east of the Sierras began to dry up.

As Lake Owens vanished, another message in the *Times* bore the title, "The Valley of Broken Hearts." A counter-campaign was launched to demonize the people of Owens Valley as selfish hoarders standing in the way of water desperately needed in progressive Los Angeles. With its supply quadrupled, the growing metropolis saw local land values rocketing to record heights.

William Mulholland, the Irish engineer who made all this possible, had started his career in Los Angeles as a ditch digger who gradually worked his way up. By the time he was chief of Water and Power, he understood that Los Angeles needed water to sustain its growth. His claims that LA was running out of water made his colleagues wealthy once the land boom in the San Fernando Valley ran rivers of money into their bank accounts.

His own triumph was not to last. When the St. Francis Dam he had supervised collapsed in 1928, sending a seventy-five-foot-high wall of water through Ventura County to kill hundreds of people, he pretended at first that terrorists had dynamited it, but nobody bought it for long. He resigned in disgrace.

Meanwhile, Los Angeles grew....and grew....and grew so much that, with water now truly in short supply, the city reached out for Mono Lake....

Contemporary history is filled with examples of how the application of mechanical thinking to complicated situations tends to unbalance them even more. In Los Angeles, making water available only encouraged the kind of massive, sprawling development that would eclipse future water supplies, just as adding lanes to a crowded freeway can encourage sprawl that results in further overcrowding.

This error of ignoring how systemic factors intermesh and mutually reinforce becomes even more obvious in dealings with the natural world. A farmer who loses 10% of a crop to an invasive bug decides to fix the problem by purchasing a pesticide from Monsanto. He sprays the crop, and for a season or two the pesticide seems to work.

Unfortunately for the farmer, however, the spray never kills all the invasive bugs. It merely eliminates the weakest, leaving the strong survivors to overbreed to compensate the loss of their population. Meanwhile the spray has also killed the beneficial bugs who eat the invasives. In another few seasons, the farmer finds he is now losing 95% of his crop to a hardier super bug freed from the check and balance of predation, immune to his handy new pesticide, and very, very hungry.

Stadiums around the U.S. switched from grass turf to plastic in order to save water, only to find that the plastic retained deadly bacteria requiring more water to clean off after each game than the original grass had drunk.

Using mechanical, linear, single-solution thinking to fix a complex living system almost always further destabilizes it.

18 - Lenin:
"Meet the New Boss...."

It's easy to see why someone like Vladimir Ilyich Ulyanov would be a reformer. Born in 1870 in a politically repressive Russia, he grew up with two politically involved educators for parents and an older anarchist brother hanged for plotting to bomb theTsar. His sister was exiled for her part in that plot. All this made a revolutionary of Lenin (see Chapter 5), who was expelled from the University of Kazan for participating in Berkeley-style student uprisings. In spite of this he earned his law degree in an off-campus program offered by the University of St. Petersburg.

In between legal tomes he had read Marx and Engels and translated the entire *Communist Manifesto* into Russian. After briefly practicing law he switched to radical politics.

This soon brought him into collision with the authorities. For engaging in revolutionary activities, he was sent to Siberia for five years. After this he began using the pseudonym "Lenin" in his writings, nicknaming himself after a large river (the Lena) in Siberia.

As Lenin traveled for fifteen years through urban Europe to collect followers, he puzzled about a central thesis of Marxism: that of an "inevitable" proletarian revolt. Yet if class-conscious laborers would eventually overthrow their capitalist masters, why had this not happened in Russia? Was it because most of the laborers were agrarian peasants rather than, say, factory workers? If so, a way must be found to take them into revolution—to convert workers into proletarians—without pausing long, if at all, in the transitional stage of capitalism. This in turn meant organizing a "revolutionary vanguard" of cultural and political elites who could guide them, watching carefully to prevent seduction by the liberals or the bourgeoisie.

Having come to these conclusions, Lenin published the influential pamphlet *What Is to be Done?* (1902) and separated himself from those in the Russian Social Democratic Labor Party, a party he had helped organize, who called for change from below rather than from above. In 1903, he put together the *Bolshevik* ("Bigger," meaning majority) wing of the RSDLP in order to sharpen his vanguard in preparation for the next phase.

The Bolsheviks began publishing *Pravda* ("Truth") in 1912 to build an effective insurrectionist propaganda, part of which was Lenin's *April Theses* attacking the Russian provisional government that took over after the Tsar abdicated. By 1917 he was arguing that a communist state should be led by a "dictatorship of the proletariat" to avoid the lures of capitalism.

In Russia, millions of people weary from World War I shivered and went hungry as the economy failed. Encouraged by this, Lenin organized the Bolsheviks for an armed uprising: the October Revolution in which a coup overthrew Alexander Krensky. The Bolsheviks were now in charge.

They wasted little time. In a matter of weeks, Russia had

withdrawn from the war, all land was under state control, and Bolshevik leaders of the Russian Communist Party were knitting together local workers councils ("soviets") to exert administrative control. An insurrection led by the White Army was put down by the Red. Lenin became head of state. So leaky was the ship of state, however, that Lenin's New Economic Policy allowed trade with foreign businesses as well as limited buying and selling of produce.

By 1918, the Bolsheviks were rigging and closing down elections promised to "the people," violently putting down opposition, and forming the Cheka, a force of secret police and assassins. Very quickly the self-appointed liberators were taking on the worst habits of the former oppressors.

On August 30, socialist revolutionary Fanya Kaplan put two bullets into Lenin. He lived, but the slugs remained lodged in his upper body. The Soviet government responded by confiscating grain, torturing and executing thousands of "enemies of the State," and sending thousands more into a labor camp system known as the terrible GULAG: the "Chief Administration of Corrective Labor Camps and Colonies."

Damage caused by the assassination attempt undoubtedly contributed to the strokes Lenin now suffered. Ongoing opposition, dissatisfied workers, industrialization of the vast Soviet Union, revolts in annexed states like Georgia, and expansion of Comintern to foment international communist revolution gave him much to worry about, but he felt particularly concerned about the Communist Party's Secretary General. His written suggestions that Josef Stalin be removed from power were attributed after Lenin's death (1924) to brain damage from strokes.

After he was gone, Stalin took power and finished the work of turning the Soviet Union into the totalitarian antithesis of everything the social democrats had fought for. As a song by The Who has it, "Meet the new boss/Same as the old boss."

The weed seeds of reform imposed from above or brought from outside sprout into new forms of oppression.

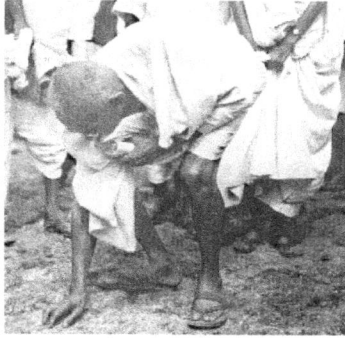

19 - Dandi:
The Strongest Mythology

After a period of waiting and uncertainty, Mohandis K. Gandhi decided to follow an "inner voice" into action.

Taxing salt provided one source of revenue for the British colonial government that ruled India. No one but the British could make or sell this precious substance freely available on every beach. Anyone caught collecting it could be fined and jailed.

On March 3, 1930, Gandhi wrote a letter to Lord Irwin, the Viceroy, to ask him to repeal the salt tax causing such economic hardship in India. "I regard this tax to be the most iniquitous of all from the poor man's standpoint." The tax was not repealed, so on March 12, Gandhi led seventy-eight marchers two hundred and forty miles from Sabarmati to the sea. By the time they arrived at Dandi on April 5th, thousands had joined along the way, marching, singing, and chanting.

The following day, after a night of prayer, Gandhi publicly and deliberately broke the law by boiling sea water to extract salt. All along the shore people eagerly followed his example. By month's end, the British had jailed 60,000 of them. Gandhi was arrested on May 4th.

Although the salt tax was not repealed until India achieved independence from British rule, it generated widespread publicity, united women and men of all economic levels and many regions, and exerted a lasting influence on future leaders of nonviolent protest, including Martin Luther King Jr. and Cesar Chavez. It taught the oppressed of India that they, not the government, held the real power.

It also demonstrated the surprising strength of an intangible but highly potent weapon in the fight for sovereignty: myth power.

Myth is not just wrong belief or an outdated way of grasping nature. The collective stories we tell ourselves about our place in the world bear a mythic structure, the only kind that can carry a persistent if mostly unconscious charge of conviction. Think about the market, or as it should be written today, the Market: served with morning rituals of calculation, guided by an "invisible hand," self-correcting, self-regulating, placed in control of the fate of millions, watched by traders who stare reverently upward at glowing screens above altar-kiosks rising from the floor of the New York Stock Exchange. Mythically speaking, the Market carries all the power of Moloch, a hungry bull god fed by the blood and currency of perpetual sacrifice.

No one believes in zombies anymore, but we do believe in the computer whose glowing monitor forehead, speechless routines, and disturbing automatisms recall the Jewish legend of the Golem created out of magically animated matter. Few sing hymns to threshold-crossing Hermes nowadays, but piles of small rocks stacked into *herms* ceremonialize many a shoreline. The primal Earth Mother peers back at us from behind environmentalist slogans about the great goddess

Gaia. The hundred-eyed watchman the Greeks spoke of as the Argus lives on in street corner camera lenses and ubiquitous electronic surveillance.

"Coincidence," we might blurt dismissively about an uncanny event or disturbing dream, convincing ourselves of our powers of reason—but in unconscious imitation of the ancient Roman habit of explaining strange events by evoking Fortuna, goddess of blind chance.

Gandhi won his long campaign in part because he wielded the more vital mythology than his opponents: that of Liberation, whereas all the stymied British managed to invoke was Order or Stability. The terms Gandhi employed radiated spiritual power; those of the British sounded musty, stiff, and propagandistic, reeking of the Home Office and not fragrant like a sacred temple. And Gandhi had salt, symbol of purification, wisdom, sweat, blood, and tears, a pure white emblem of one of nature's most crucial life-giving processes.

In 2008, Barack Obama handily won the U.S. Presidential election with a mythology of Change; his Republican opponents had little to drawn on beyond Fear and Terror, the sons of Mars. By one year into his presidency, Obama had squandered most of his myth power by turning his back on his idealistic base and, as wars raged on in Iraq and Afghanistan, pandering to the bloodthirsty followers of Phobos and Deimos.

In any sustained conflict between opposing groups, the side with the strongest mythology always wins.

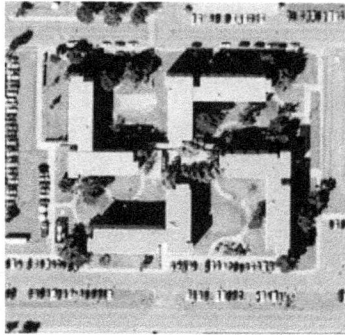

20 - Reichstag:
The Old State Security Excuse

Those who would give up essential Liberty, to purchase a little temporary Safety, deserve neither Liberty nor Safety.
> – Benjamin Franklin, 1755

On February 27, 1933, a police officer walking by the Reichstag building in Berlin smelled smoke and went to investigate. The building housed the German parliament of the Republic.

Soon the wood panels, floors, and chairs were blazing. The glass dome over the central chamber crashed down, splintering into thousands of shards, as firefighters tried to save the flaming structure. Outside the building, police spotted and arrested Communist and unemployed bricklayer Marinus van der Lubbe. When they questioned him he only grinned, but

77

when tortured claimed to have set the fire.

As smoke drifted above the remains, minister Hermann Goering ordered the arrest of a hundred Communist members of the Reichstag and shut down all "leftist" and "liberal" newspapers. It was a matter, explained the Nazis, of state security. Hitler called the fire "a sign from heaven."

Basic rights under the Constitution were then suspended, including articles guaranteeing private property, privacy of communications, personal liberty, freedom of the press, and the right to hold meetings not authorized by the government. The purpose, Hitler argued, was to combat "terror." Those suspected of terrorist activities—namely, activists, pacifists, and "Reds"—were detained indefinitely without legal representation. "Nothing is being left unsaid and undone," noted the *New York Times* on February 28th, "to arouse a wave of popular hysteria in advance of Sunday's elections." These were parliamentary elections called by Hitler in order to establish a legislative Nazi majority.

In March of 1933, bullied Reichstag members voted that Hitler's cabinet could make its own laws without consulting anyone but itself. According to this well-named Enabling Act, "Federal laws may be enacted by the government [Hitler's Cabinet] outside of the procedure provided in the Constitution...." Newspapers in Germany blared that in the government's opinion, the state was in danger and continued to be.

With a nation of frightened people behind him, a nation smarting from military defeat and a plunging economy, Hitler found it easy to wield his "blood and soil" mythology for his own genocidal purposes. A priority high on his list was establishing a Department of Fatherland Security, an organization with the initials S.S. Its aim, the Nazis explained, was to watch over state security.

When the U.S. Congress passed the illegal and immoral Indian Appropriations Act (1851) to place Native Americans on reservations, it did this, politicians explained to the public, to protect the Indians—and to guard state security.

When Vladimir Lenin ordered the new Red Army into action against "insurrectionists" (1919), he said it was to maintain state security.

When Josef Stalin initiated the Great Purge (1936) that killed thousands of "traitors," he used the same excuse: state security.

When Joseph McCarthy called for purges of Reds (1950) and began wrecking the careers of thousands of innocent Americans (see Chapter 25), he too invoked it: state security.

That year the Republic of South Africa passed the Group Areas Act to legalize apartheid. Why? "State security," and the need to fight off "terrorists" who disagreed with government policy.

Suspension of democracy in Burma, 1962: state security.

Tiananmen Square, 1989: state security.

Post-September 11, 2001 suspension of habeus corpus, communications privacy, and a long list of other formerly guaranteed rights: state security.

When organized extremists make an extra-legal bid for total power, their excuse is always the same: state security.

21 - Manzanar:
The Persistence of Paranoia

<u>Executive Order No. 9066</u>

...By virtue of the authority vested in me as President of the United States, and Commander in Chief of the Army and Navy, I hereby authorize and direct the Secretary of War...to prescribe military areas in such places and of such extent as he or the appropriate Military Commander may determine, from which any or all persons may be excluded, and with respect to which, the right of any person to enter, remain in, or leave shall be subject to whatever restrictions the Secretary of War or the appropriate Military Commander may impose in his discretion....

Over the objections of his wife, President Franklin Roosevelt signed this order in 1942 at the instigation of Lieutenant General John De Witt of the Western Defense Command.

The precipitating events were the shelling of a Santa Barbara oil refinery by a Japanese submarine that missed its target, a false report of Japanese planes over San Francisco, and a mysterious outbreak of anti-aircraft gunfire over Los Angeles. De Witt had this to say in 1943 about uprooting 120,000 Japanese citizens from their homes and sending them into internment without trials or even accusations:

> The evacuation was impelled by military necessity [i.e. state security]. The security of the Pacific Coast continues to require the exclusion of Japanese from the area now prohibited to them [why was never specified] and will so continue as long as that military necessity exists...Intelligence services records reflected the existence of hundreds of Japanese organizations in California, Washington, Oregon, and Arizona which, prior to December 7, 1941, were actively engaged in advancing Japanese war aims [no such organizations existed]. These records also disclosed that thousands of American-born Japanese had gone to Japan to receive their education and indoctrination there and had become rabidly pro-Japanese [no evidence for this ever came to light] and then had returned to the United States.

After the war De Witt was promoted to the rank of full general.

With the Japanese now targeted, pretend patriots came out of the woodwork like angered earwigs. The Lions and Elks, the

Townsend Club, numerous agricultural and business groups, various chambers of commerce, the American Legion, Governor Olson of California, Attorney General Earl Warren, Mayor Angelo Rossi of San Francisco, Fletcher Bowron of Los Angeles, Senators Hiram Johnson and Sheridan Downey, the *LA Times*, the entire California State Assembly, the California Joint Immigration Committee, the Native Sons and Daughters of the Golden West: all got behind the demonization of Japanese Americans as subversives, traitors, and terrorists.

Over a six-month period, the Western Defense Command moved these people into assembly centers where they were tagged and documented before being detained in ten relocation sites—in other words, prisons—in six states. No charges were ever filed. No one had the right to appeal their confinement. The U.S. Supreme Court upheld the legality of this confinement when it was finally challenged. Meanwhile, 30,000 Japanese American soldiers and sailors fought for freedom in distant lands.

The indignity of this loss of liberty echoed down the generations. Some of the inmates died while incarcerated. Property loss came to around $1.3 billion, and income loss to $2.7 billion.

In the dehydrated wastes of the Owens Valley stood Camp Manzanar not far from where Paiutes had been massacred by settlers and where the oligarchs of Los Angeles had drained Lake Owens nearly dry. "Each block," reported Jean Wakatsuki Houston, who was confined there as a child, "was built to the same design....built to a common master plan." Today nothing is left out there but a monument and a wooden guard tower with its back to the snowy heights of the Sierras.

Yet in spite of this dreadful legacy of betrayal, jingoism, and hatred masquerading as patriotism, paranoia remains rampant in politics. In the U.S., where people of Arab descent have been denounced, fingerprinted, and racially profiled since 9/11, members of Congress have called for deportation of Iranians as recently as 2009. Politicians and talk show hosts foment intolerance and fear by throwing around labels like "terrorist," "traitor," "socialist," and "liberal." Hate sells, profitably.

Psychologically, paranoia can be understood as a mental projection of violent impulses onto convenient external targets. Accusations made carelessly and without careful substantiation echo unerringly the accuser's mentality: Hitler accusing the Allies of wanting to take over the world (his own project), for example, or Pieter Botha accusing the African National Conference of wanting to spread terror (his own agenda). Public figures who call for witch hunts and loyalty pledges are themselves guilty of unweaving the fabric of trust, confidence, and decency that holds communities together.

Those who level paranoid accusations harbor a toxic rage that undermines social structures the accusers say they support.

22 - Rommel:
The Revolt of Neglected Talent

Born in Heidenheim, Germany, in 1891, Erwin Rommel Jr. seemed to have walked into a charmed life. As the second son of a schoolmaster, he emerged from a pleasant childhood to excel in school, marry a lifelong companion, and raise a son who became a mayor. A dutiful son himself, he obeyed his father's wish to stop studying engineering. Instead, he entered the military academy.

During World War I Rommel survived several risky operations and earned himself promotions, commendations, an Iron Cross, and the respect of his peers and commanding officers. His book on infantry tactics, written for his academy students, also instructed Adolf Hitler, who made Rommel part of his personal guard. Rommel's acute intelligence and confidence made a stark if unvoiced contrast to the jarring insecurity of Hitler, whose childhood had been anything but happy and secure. Yet Rommel trusted and obeyed the Führer enough to command one of the first Panzer attacks of World War II.

Was it because of Hitler's uncanny charisma? The spell cast by charisma wears off. Rommel had been raised in a Protestant home that glorified family values, patriotic duty, rigid discipline, and obedience to authority. By the time he questioned this early programming, he was too late to save himself from its final consequences.

Even in his school years Rommel's creative versatility and penetrating boldness had astonished instructors and students alike. At the opening of World War II, his tank force swept forward in an armored thrust that caught the French unprepared and encircled them before they knew it. The deciding factor lay not in equipment—his opponents fielded well-armored tanks with large-caliber guns—but in speed, audacity, and inventiveness. With their minds trapped by the entrenchment ideology of World War I, the French generals could not keep up with Rommel's new type of cavalry.

Decorated and promoted once again, Rommel then flew off to Africa, where he commanded the fabled Afrika Korps in alliance with Italians fighting against the British in Tunisia and Libya. The year was 1941.

It must have felt to him as though the desert wind and sun somehow tightened the red tape he had always complained about. Because the High Command never sent him enough men or supplies, he found himself nearly always outnumbered. Often he would stage a brilliant attack, only to find that a supporting force comprised of Italians or his own men ended up besieged, broken down, or lost in the sands. Sketchy Wehrmacht air support only multiplied the danger. In letters to his wife, Rommel railed openly at incompetent Italian leadership, inadequate German support, and what he thought of as the quartermaster mentality's plodding predilection for making prompt action difficult. Religious sentiments buoyed him up: "I have complete faith that God is keeping a protective hand over us and that He will grant us victory."

At first Rommel did well in Africa. With the ready-handed-ness of Daedalus, flying architect of Olympus, he struck suddenly into enemy weak spots scouted from an airplane flown through storms. Feinting an attack here or there, he followed up elsewhere, stunning his opponents. Aircraft propellers mounted on the backs of trucks blew huge clouds of dust that made his mobile forces seem larger than they were. Several times he evaded capture by a hair's breadth, once by stealing a British armored car. When the British staged a strong armored counterattack, Rommel redeployed antiaircraft guns to pick off oncoming tanks.

Up to a point, Rommel was willing to overlook the irrationalities of the High Command, even when they ordered him to kill any Jews he captured (he refused). What he could not tolerate was official disregard for what he offered. Again and again he made a well-reasoned case for strengthening German forces in Africa as a prelude to dominating the entire Mediterranean, only to receive the bureaucratic rebuffs that infuriated him. "The only military thinking which was acceptable," he wrote in his road journal, "was that which followed their standardised rules. Everything outside the rules was regarded as a gamble...." He knew he deserved better than he received from functionaries who could only say "nein."

The breakthrough came when Rommel returned from Africa after being vastly outnumbered and outgunned and never equipped with sufficient supplies or men. When he tried to explain this to Hitler, who had once promoted him to the rank of field marshal, the Führer threw a tantrum and blamed Rommel's men for not fighting hard enough. Visualizing them in P.O.W. camps, listening to his commander raving about defeated soldiers deserving death, Rommel finally lost his idealization of a madman capable, the Desert Fox now saw, of sacrificing the entirety of Germany rather than sue for peace.

The result was predictable. When a colleague quietly asked for his allegiance in a plot to kill Hitler, Rommel disagreed with the method—death would only magnify the mad Führer's influence—but decided to offer what help he could by reaching out to the Allies with an offer of peace.

How often loyal commanders come to bad ends, with relatively few—James Wolfe at Quebec, Lord Nelson at Trafalgar, Gustavus Adolphus at Lützen—dying in battle. Stilicho and Scipio Africanus, Rome's two greatest generals, died bitterly estranged from the ungrateful governments they had served. Waldstein, Shaka, and Caesar were assassinated. Grant and Lee fared better in old age, but Thomas "Stonewall" Jackson, more talented by far than either, was killed by friendly fire at age thirty-nine. Hannibal and Boudica poisoned themselves to avoid worse fates, Bonaparte was poisoned by someone else, as might have been Alexander (unless he simply drank himself to death), and Joan of Arc was handed over by those she had fought for to be burned at the stake by their enemies. William Wallace fared still worse: he was captured, tried, beaten, dragged around town by a horse, beaten again, hanged briefly, castrated, eviscerated, and finally beheaded and quartered.

Rommel was found out, denounced, and as a national hero offered a gentleman's private choice: take poison and die with his family cared for and his reputation intact, or be executed as a traitor with the fate of his wife and son sealed as well. Rommel took the poison, and his executioners kept their word. One of his accusers, General Guderian, had driven victoriously across France with him. Guderian was eventually relieved by Hitler during a heated disagreement about tank strategy.

Many historical lessons can be culled from these events, one of which is this:

The talented exiled by the arrogant and ignorant often returns, but as a dangerous enemy.

23 - Trinity:
Promethean Enthusiasm

It seems eerily appropriate that the nuclear age erupted out on the Jornada del Muerto, the fabled "Journey (or Route) of Death," a shield-shaped road of lava along which so many thirsty travelers had died in the desert. An old legend has it that Bernardo Gruber, a trader nicknamed "El Aleman" ("The German"), was arrested in 1666 by Inquisitors for bragging about some witchcraft he had been taught. He escaped into the Jornada and vanished, no one knew exactly where until searchers came across a skull, bones, and hair. Near this odd foreshadowing of radiation attack a cross was erected. Oppenheimer called his test site Trinity.

Robert J. Oppenheimer was a graduate of the New York School of Ethical Culture. As "Coordinator of Rapid Rupture," he led a team of thirty young scientists to Los Alamos in 1942 to secretly construct the world's first atomic bomb.

From the start (according to scientists present at the time), a mysterious, reckless mania gripped the team: a rush to create that only intensified when they learned that the Germans had fallen far behind in their own attempts to forge an atomic weapon. Scientists worked long hours, partied, pulled bizarre practical jokes, slept with prostitutes. A betting pool offered guesses about the bomb's destructive power spanning zero results to vaporization of the entire planet: no one knew for sure what would happen when the nuclear trigger was pulled. To relieve the mad pace, technicians concocted dangerous drinks out of laboratory alcohol.

Strange accidents plagued the project: a near-meltdown when scientists who dubbed themselves the Cowpuncher Committee "tickled the dragons tail," an accidental bombing of Trinity Base Camp by trainee pilots aiming for running antelope, malfunctioning detonators, cracked lens moulds, consumption of tainted camp water, another risky overheating as masked men bending over the bomb like surgeons at a delivery tried to get the core to fit into the assembly.....

On July 16th, 1945, the day of the test, lightning played around the bomb tower as though the elements themselves protested the imminent tearing asunder of nature's constitutive fabric. Despite more last-moment glitches, the bomb erupted with a blast so bright that a blind woman saw it from miles down the highway. "Now we are all sons of bitches," somberly remarked physicist Kenneth Bainbridge. Invisible fallout drifted down over nearby ranches whose owners had been kept in the dark about the terrible technological monster brought to life in their midst.

On August 6th, the United States Government, having refused to withdraw its demand that the Japanese surrender unconditionally, issued an order, and a uranium bomb dropped from the air destroyed the city of Hiroshima. A second weapon devastated Nagasaki two days later. In each case most of the destruction took less than ten seconds.

Oppenheimer and other Manhattan Project scientists

began to feel a delayed sense of remorse and horror over this use of their creation against civilian targets, but it was too late, as Oppenheimer came to realize: the atomic monster, assembled part by part like Frankenstein's lethal beast, had been set loose among humankind. A spy at Los Alamos gave the secret of its construction to the Russians.

Why did a group of brilliant, humanitarian, and moderately liberal scientists create this weapon of mass destruction?

Writer Francis Ferguson, a friend of Oppenheimer, recalled that "....he was extremely ignorant about practical matters, and he didn't care about them. His whole life was in the intellect." A recurring motif in the lives of scientists who do not pause to reflect on the potential consequences of their creations. So is this: "The dream had somehow got hold of him," observed physicist Freeman Dyson. "The Faustian bargain is when you sell your soul to the devil in exchange for knowledge and power....When once you sell your soul to the devil, there's no going back on it."

Physicist Robert Wilson reported that he and the other researchers felt like "automatons" who had been "directed to do one thing." In retrospect he could not understand why he failed to walk away from the project once the Germans surrendered. A brief team discussion about the morality of what they were building was submerged beneath another wave of work. Frank Oppenheimer, who was also among them, said afterward, "Amazing, how the technology, tools, trap one. They're so powerful....When VE day came along, no one slowed down one bit....The machinery had caught us...."

In Mary Shelley's predictive novel *Frankenstein: A Modern Prometheus*, the inventive doctor represents the epitome of clean and clear rationality. Science, not superstition, will make humanity immortal, he is certain. Failing to recognize this as a religious aspiration (the spirit's heavenward ascent away from body and earth: a monotheistic dream dressed up in scientific garb), the doctor gives form not to salvation, but damnation. The dark inner impulses his idealized intellectualism denies to consciousness contaminate his research. Only when it ends does he realize his ghastly mistake. In wielding the tools of the creator god (hence "Prometheus" in the subtitle), by taking over the exclusively feminine prerogative of giving birth, he has equipped his denied irrationality--the monstrous, death-loving shadow of creative Prometheus--with a body strong enough to break bones and murder loved ones. The machinery had caught him.

As part of its 2011 President's Budget, the U.S. Department of Defense proposes a project called BioDesign. Its mission is to eliminate "the randomness of natural evolutionary advancement." Never mind that natural selection isn't random, but a fitting of organisms into earthly ecosystems worked out over billions of years. How will this elimination be done? By creating creatures genetically engineered to "produce the intended biological effect," whatever that is: presumably one that is militarily advantageous. The creatures will be programmed to be loyal, reliable—and immortal. They will come with a molecular "kill switch" to make sure they remain under Pentagon control.

> You seek for knowledge and wisdom, as I once did; and I ardently hope that the gratification of your wishes may not be a serpent to sting you, as mine has been. I do not know that the relation of my disasters will be useful to you; yet, when I reflect that you are pursuing the same course, exposing yourself to the same dangers which have rendered me what I am, I imagine that you may deduce an apt moral from my tale...
> – Victor Frankenstein

Ignoring the shadows and monsters within us enlarges them externally into gigantic, dangerous creations.

24 - Watson:
Push-Button Cures

"HAS PSYCHOLOGY LOST ITS MIND?" asked the title of a paper presented by William Montague in 1912. Many would wonder that in years to come. Montague was writing to critique a trend in the field that reduced all of human action and interiority to shaped stimuli and response.

America's self-authorized expert on behavior and child-rearing was born in South Carolina in 1878, the fourth of six children and the son of a violent and promiscuous drunk who abandoned his family. They were fundamentalist Baptists who had lost their wealth during the Civil War, and as a boy, John Watson seems to have channeled this family resentment by beating up black kids on his way to school. Once there he did poorly and was often in trouble, but even then he showed a turn for ambition. At age sixteen he entered Furman University, a college for ministers. (Quite a few pioneering psychologists received their undergraduate training as idealistic clergymen.)

Having earned his PhD at the University of Chicago, where he dropped philosophy in favor of science in part because he disliked John Dewey's emphasis on self-direction and inner growth, Watson gained an appointment as professor of experimental psychology at Johns Hopkins. While there he seems to have suffered some kind of breakdown, panic attacks perhaps. He built rat mazes despite psychologist James Angell's doubt that rats could tell Watson anything important about human motivation. To get around the rules against romance with students, he assumed a false name in order to wed Mary Ickes, which he did while continuing to see a former lover. His belief in the Progress of Man combined with square-chinned looks that might have adorned the lecturing hero of an Ayn Rand novel to make him an object of feminine attention.

All animals, he came to believe, were complex machines (as Descartes had thought) responding to various situations in accord with their "wiring": neural pathways conditioned by experience. Humans were no different, just a bit more complex. In 1913 he published "Psychology as the Behaviorist Views It," an article that broke from the dominant focus on internal processes. For Watson, psychology should keep to the goal of what he had never enjoyed in childhood: prediction and control. It should forget about the world-within and shed light on what could be quantified: namely, outer behavior. (As an adult Watson slept with his light on at night, a habit he probably attributed to early training instead of to fear of some scary darkness still alive within himself....)

Watson remained at John Hopkins until 1920, when his academic career ended with a scandal made public by a love letter from Rosalie Raynor, a student and research assistant roughly half his age. Raynor's wealthy Baltimore family donated money to the university. Watson's wife had intercepted the letter. The university asked him to resign.

From there he went into advertising. By 1924 he was vice

president at J. Walter Thompson, where he pioneered the use of celebrity endorsements, brand loyalty (to Yuban first, then Camel, Johnson's Baby Powder, and Ponds), impulse buying, timed obsolescence, and instilling consumers with a constant craving for new commodities. It would stretch no truth to say that Watson and Edward Bernays, the nephew of Freud, founded mass advertising by supplying it with a psychological arsenal to be used against the consumer.

In 1928 Watson wrote *The Psychological Care of the Infant Child* to advise parents that good behaviorist fathers and mothers must be more regimental than affectionate, starting with taking the child from mother in the third or fourth week of life. When older,

> Children should be awakened at 6:30 A.M. for orange juice and a pee. Play 'till 7:30. Breakfast should be at 7:30 sharp; at 8:00 they should be placed on the toilet for twenty minutes or less 'til bowel movement is complete. Then follow up with a verbal report. The child would then play indoors 'till 10:00 A.M., after 10:00 outside, a short nap after lunch, then "social play" with others. In the evening a bath, quiet play until bedtime at 8:00 sharp.

Watson's own son described him as "unresponsive, emotionally uncommunicative, unable to express and cope with any feelings or emotions of his own…" His wife Rosalie publicly disagreed with her husband, but at home she towed the party line.

After her death, Watson retreated from public life. As a recluse he lived in a farmhouse that resembled his family home, finally drinking himself into the grave in 1958. His legacy included a daughter, Polly, who attempted suicide several times, and a granddaughter, actress Mariette Hartley, who talked about him in her book *Breaking the Silence:* "Grandfather's theories infected my mother's life, my life, and the lives of millions. How do you break a legacy? How do you keep from passing a debilitating inheritance down, generation to generation, like a genetic flaw?" In 1930, Watson, who had conditioned a boy ("Little Albert") to fear furry creatures, had boasted with Promethean glee:

> Give me a dozen healthy infants, well-formed, and my own specified world to bring them up in and I'll guarantee to take any one at random and train him to become any type of specialist I might select—doctor, lawyer, artist, merchant-chief and, yes, even beggar-man and thief, regardless of his talents, penchants, tendencies, abilities, vocations, and race of his ancestors.

And so a variant of the American self-made man, in this case made by someone else.

Behaviorism's focus on the mechanical and measurable aspects of human nature gave it appeal for researchers more comfortable with machinery than with messy inner lives. It was relatively simple. It avoided the effort of toiling in the service of self-knowledge. It relieved the sense of personal responsibility (the environment made me do it). It promised limited and obtainable concrete goals. It placed authority in the hands of expert behavior technicians. It elevated conformism to a norm. And it encouraged a consumerist model of the person—programmable, predictable, easily led—that allowed it to be imported directly into advertising and political propagandizing "beyond freedom and dignity," as the title of B.F. Skinner's book expressed it.

For the most part behavioral psychology has gone out of fashion, although treatment programs continue to employ it here and there, with mixed results. (People have a way of protesting this kind of objectification by subverting "prediction and control.") But the behavioral emphasis on quick fixes and techno-cures never dissipated. Today, thousands who would laugh at behaviorist mechanicality engage in daily psychological plastic surgery by subjecting themselves to an unending regimen of cleansings, cleanings, purifications, purgings, eye rollings, sacred movements, contemplations, meditations, affirmations, and various outer and inner diets. Salvation is always around the corner, a brand new self waiting on the doorstep like a package just delivered.

Few suspect that the healing methods themselves might pathologize, depriving their adherents of the internal space and stillness necessary for bearing the emotional weight of human imperfection, or that the real agenda is not healing but, as with the behaviorists, prediction and control.

As a result, sore spots and unhappinesses that body and mind might have healed on their own persist for years and even get worse. A lesson, then, in lieu of quick cures:

To find resolution, deep hurts and conflicts must be lived through consciously until they reveal how constant fiddling stops them from healing themselves.

25 - McCarthy:
When Silence Means Complicity

On January 7, 1950, four men met for dinner at the Colony Restaurant in Washington D.C. as a cold winter wind roared outside: William Roberts, attorney; Edmund Walsh, a Jesuit from Georgetown University; Charles Kraus, a professor of politics also from Georgetown U; and Senator Joseph McCarthy.

McCarthy had cause for concern: an upcoming election. A mediocre Senator, he was being investigated for cheating on his taxes, lying about his war record, and taking bribes from PepsiCola. On his first day as a senator he had called for ending a coal strike by drafting the strikers and shooting them for insubordination. He needed, he told the group, an electrifying and relevant issue with which to promote himself.

After some discussion, Father Walsh offered that McCarthy might successfully accuse Democrats and liberals of being

Communists. "That's it," said McCarthy, a former Democrat who angrily switched parties after failing to be appointed the Democratic Party choice for district attorney.

Up until this opportunity, McCarthy, an unsuccessful lawyer, slandered his opponents primarily by means of innuendo, implying that they were too old, corrupt, or unpatriotic to serve in high office. His new strategy drew on his past as a gambler. Standing before the Republican Women's Club in Wheeling, Virginia on February 9, 1950, he claimed to have a list of two hundred and five secret Communist Party members in the State Department. That he never produced such a list and kept changing its numbers would not trip him up until the end of four years of smear-based terror now known as McCarthyism.

After winning the election by accusing several Democrats of subversive activity and others of being soft on Communism, McCarthy proceeded to destroy the careers not only of politicians, but of artists, writers, actors, journalists, broadcasters, and educators. Many were jailed on totally unsubstantiated charges. Others left the country. One of these, Thomas Mann, had emigrated to the U.S. to escape German fascism. In 1952 he left for Switzerland, writing,

> We can already see the first signs of terrorism, talebearing, political inquisition, and suspension of law, all of which are excused by an alleged state of emergency. As a German I can only say: That is the way it began among us, too.

After McCarthy published a list of "Communist" and "un-American" books available in libraries, the books were removed from the shelves. Had it been published then, Arthur Miller's play *After the Fall*, a thoughtful study of accomplice psychology, would surely have been included. Before leaving the country Thomas Mann had published *Doctor Faustus*, a novel about a man who sold his soul to the devil and went mad.

Had McCarthy left the paranoia he had triggered to do its poisonous work, his false front as patriot and national hero might have remained intact a little longer, but, drunk with power as well as with alcohol, he went too far. When his list of traitors and subversives expanded to include the Secretary of State, the President's speech writer, former Assistant Secretary of State William Benton, and the Secretary of the Army, McCarthy was finally censured in the Senate (December 2, 1954) and removed from the chairmanship of the Government Committee on Operations of the Senate. President Eisenhower, a Republican elected in part because of fear drummed up by McCarthy, nodded approvingly.

Those who had been afraid to speak now came forward with loud denunciations. His credibility gone, McCarthy lost his voice as newspapers, radio stations, and television shows did what they should have done to start with and stopped paying attention to him, broadcasting him, or publishing his writings. He died in 1957 of an inflamed liver. He was forty-eight years old.

After he died, thousands of secret cables wired back and forth between U.S. and Soviet spies were finally deciphered in the 1990s by U.S. intelligence. Did this "Venona Project" vindicate McCarthy? Far from it, according to Professor Harvey Klehr, who studied the archives. "....There is little evidence," he told a conference in Raleigh, "that those he fingered were among the unidentified spies of Venona."

Klehr continued:

> Many of his claims were wildly inaccurate; his charges filled with errors of fact, misjudgments of organizations and innuendoes disguised as evidence. He failed to recognize or understand the differences among genuine liberals, fellow-traveling liberals,

Communist dupes, Communists and spies — distinctions that were important to make. The new information from Russian and American archives does not vindicate McCarthy. He remains a demagogue, whose wild charges actually made the fight against Communist subversion more difficult.

Not everyone had been intimidated by McCarthy. Journalists like Edward Murrow, George Seldes, John Steinbeck, and I.F. Stone, comedians like Mort Sahl ("If you maintain a consistent political position for long enough, you will eventually be accused of treason"), and playwrights like Arthur Miller had come forward from early on to speak up against McCarthyism at the risk of being blacklisted.

Nevertheless, McCarthy succeeded at his extended bout of gambling for as long as he did because the very people who should have denounced his lies and smear tactics remained silent for too long, some afraid that they too would be accused of being traitors. Instead of standing up to him, exposing his motives and investigating his character and tactics, they withdrew, and thereby became his quiet accomplices. Without such no paranoiac madman succeeds for long.

The lessons of Salem (see Chapter 12), the Reichstag fire (Chapter 20), and Manzanar (Chapter 21) had gone unlearned, and so had this one:

Spreaders of intimidation, slander, and fear grow louder until they are seen through and denounced.

26 - Maharishi:
The Movable Ego

In the late 1950s, various "gurus" raised in the Far East but trained in Western schools began touring the world teaching it how to be enlightened. Some were martial artists (with Bruce Lee a later and notable exception, believing as he did that the Western arts could be more practical for self-defense than the "fancy mess" taught abroad). Most, however, were linen-wrapped wise men well aware of a widespread hunger for magic solutions (see Chapter 24) to inner and outer problems.

Like many who would adulterate Zen, Vedanta, Yoga, and other Eastern disciplines for mass appeal, Maharishi Mahesh was born in Asia but given a thoroughly Western education. He never liked talking about his past, but he did claim an undergraduate degree in physics and evidently did some fac-tory work before plunging into the spiritual classics of Hinduism. Of his 1958 world tour friendly newspapers claimed that no money was sought, for "his worldly possessions can be carried in one hand": a strange claim indeed about the man who would find the effrontery to ask Los Angeles for $165 million a year for five years and who would own a fleet of Rolls Royce cars one day. In 1959 he began teaching meditation in the United States.

Maharishi's claims were nothing if not grandly stated. He claimed that what he called Transcendental Meditation—internally repeating a syllable in Sanskrit to oneself over and over—would initiate world peace, cure poverty, grant long life, and improve health. Later research would partially support the health claim, showing that meditation brought calmness and other benefits, especially when combined with exercise and a sensible diet. But when his claims included invisibility, mind-reading, immortality, and "yogic flying" (which turned out to be bouncing on one's rump across a yoga mat), he got the attention of the Beatles, who visited his ashram in India in 1968. After a few weeks they left as rumors circulated of Maharishi's attempts to seduce young women in the entourage. According to another version of the story, he evicted the Fabulous Four for drug use. "We're leaving," Lennon told him according to one account. Lennon liked to speak his mind. "If you're so cosmic, you'll know why."

Whatever the truth of the matter, Maharishi was now the celebrities' guru: not only Mia Farrow (who had complained about his amorous touch but retracted), but Shirley MacLaine, Vidal Sassoon, Mick Jagger, the Beach Boys, David Lynch, and even Kurt Vonnegut appeared for instruction in the higher arts of transformative bliss. Comedians began to parody the Teacher's extravagantly luxurious lifestyle.

Now based in Hollywood, where his messianic persona could reach its full scope, Maharishi founded a Spiritual Regeneration Movement, in effect a transnational corporation complete with trusts, universities, the Heaven on Earth property company, a consulting business to advise architects how to design things spiritually, various health clinics, firms selling products like massage oils, books, videos, and spiritual therapy, Peace Palaces so people could produce beneficial effects locally, and subscription satellite TV programming in twenty-two languages. By 1988, Maharishi, having declared other spiritual paths obsolete, came up with a "master plan"—called "natural government" in California, where a Natural Law Party sprang up full of mystifying optimism—for evolving a worldwide utopia free of crime and sorrow.

For some time now, the architect of this empire of happiness had vanished behind barbed wire into his compound, a former Franciscan monastery situated in the Netherlands. He said he was devoting his time to silence and further study, if not to a Castanedan avoidance of debate and confrontation, but his reach remained wholly undiminished. In 1993, Maharishi placed an ad in the *Los Angeles Times* asking for money to save Los Angeles from violence and disharmony. ("Jesus only asked for a few loaves of bread and some fish," chuckled columnist Al Martinez, "but then I guess he wasn't up against Uzis and AK-47s.")

In 2004, the reedy voice from the Netherlands ordered followers to beam love and good thoughts at Tony Blair, who evidently needed them after supporting the disastrous war in Iraq, and at George W. Bush, chief instigator of that war. When nothing happened, Maharishi had the faithful direct the "beautiful nectar" of their devotional energies elsewhere.

At present, this claim adorns the website of the Maharishi School of the Age of Enlightenment:

> Scientific research [?] has established that the group practice of the Transcendental Meditation and TM-Sidhi® programs, including Yogic Flying, on a sufficiently large scale (the square root of 1% of a population) is the most powerful peace-creating technology.

> Until now, the only alternatives have been
> discussion, negotiation, and peace treaties,
> none of which have created lasting world
> peace.

The square root of 1%? Not 1.2% 2.5%?

A glance at actual world history paints quite a different picture of the matter. Discussion, dialog, negotiation, and patient treaty work: nothing has ever replaced these as instruments for halting war. As for meditation, it's been humming along steadily for centuries in India, where it has utterly failed to cure unremitting bloodshed, widespread poverty, disease, classism, sexism, racism, religious intolerance, or ecological destruction; in China, which quivers under the combat boot of a "people's republic" standing firmly on its neck; or even in the United States, where civil liberties wither under bellicose posturing and mass surveillance as distracted citizens hang Tibetan prayer flags and light another stick of incense, hoping against hope for a nicer world but satisfied for now at being submerged in so immense a network of goodness and light. A network in which the highly displaceable ego has found a new incarnation in structures of massification larger than itself.

As for the wealthy Maharishi, he did teach us at least one lasting lesson, to wit:

Those who call loudest for eliminating egotism are themselves most in need of their message.

27 - Berlin:
"Every wall is a door."

On November 9th, 1989, after months of largely non-violent citizen protests, the government of East Germany announced that it would open the Berlin Wall for limited private travel. When news of some "historic day" or other circulated, guards at the Wall found themselves overwhelmed by hordes of people eager to pass through. Lacking instructions, the guards let them, and the flow increased, and the day became historic in fact.

The wall started out as a barbed wire fence raised at night on August 13, 1961. In time it went through three evolutions, each attempting to strengthen a permeable membrane that grew to ninety-six miles in length and twelve feet in height.

Like all walls, this one originated in a pre-existing state of division. At the end of World War II, the Allies—the United States, Great Britain, France, and the Soviet Union—carved

Germany into four zones. This left the problem of what to do with Berlin, an island of Western culture and capital surrounded by territory in Soviet hands. In 1948, the Soviets pressed their claim to Berlin by blockading travel into and out of the city, but, as the Berlin Wall itself would demonstrate, walls invite bypass. An airlift flew in supplies until the ineffectual blockade was lifted.

Since at least 1945, people had fled from economically devastated East Berlin, where the Soviets, owed war reparations, were busy confiscating billions of dollars' worth of industrial and agricultural production. Entire factories were relocated as local finance faltered and jobs disappeared. To stop the flight of three million East Berliners, the German Democratic Republic (GDR) decided to build an "anti-fascist protection wall."

The first version having proved too easy to get over and under and through, the second came with mines and clearer fields of fire for watchful snipers. The third stood on thousands of blocks of reinforced concrete. Eventually, three hundred and two watch towers and twenty bunkers guarded its length and turned their searchlights toward the no man's land of the border. Between the wall's construction in 1961 and its fall in 1989, a hundred and ninety two people lost their lives in desperate attempts to cross it.

Many succeeded, however. Some tunneled, others leaped from nearby buildings, and one family even made use of a hot air balloon. A bold driver put down the top of his convertible and raced under a raised barrier. Each time the East German military responded by futilely adding defense; apparently no one had read Emerson—"Every wall is a door"—or stumbled upon the idea of spending money instead on making East Germany a desirable place to live.

Instead, government funds poured into military spending, which rose 73.5% between 1969 and 1977. In 1981, it went up another 8.4%. Meanwhile, the GDR's international debts continued to bleed into a larger and larger deficit. Adding to the general unhappiness and lack of trust in government, the local elections of 1989 kept the official party in power despite huge popular opposition and evidence of obvious vote-rigging. Peaceful demonstrations intensified, especially after Hungary opened its borders to Austria in August. Ignoring the protests, the East German government celebrated its fortieth anniversary in October by parading military hardware through the streets.

This only made people angrier, and more joined the demonstrations, now staged at the capital itself. By this time writing was already on the wall, just as it had been when the Mongols came to the Great Wall in China and the Germans themselves to the Maginot Line, both barriers easily bypassed. The "smart wall" remains a contradiction in terms, for it originates in walls of paranoia built around the unseen hearts of the defenders.

Such was the collective passion to tear down the wall in Berlin that much of it has disappeared. Parts are still visible here and there, a salutary reminder of a crucial lesson:

Oppressive borders invite their own transgression.

28 - Gaza:
Victims and Persecutors

Gaza's resistance to conquest probably goes all the way back to its naming from root words for "strong" and "prized." Its list of temporary conquerors includes Joshua (successor to Moses), Samson (who died there), Alexander the Great, the Philistines, the Romans, the Byzantines, the Rightly-Guided Caliphate, Christian Crusaders, Mongols, the Ottomans, the British (in WW I), the Egyptians (1948), and the Israelis, who captured Gaza during the Six-Day War in 1967.

The Israelis granted limited self-government in 1994, when the Palestinian National Authority under Yasser Arafat made its headquarters in the Gaza Strip: a bone-shaped coastal sector twenty-five miles long and four to seven miles wide. Hamas ("Islamic Resistance Movement") has been in charge, more or less, since 2007.

In 2000, elements of Gaza's predominantly Palestinian Muslim population rose up (*intifada*) against ongoing Israeli occupation. By 2005, the Israelis had pulled out of their settlements and bases but continued to restrict traffic in and out of Gaza. They also raised a fortified barrier to wall in the Palestinians for purposes of "state security." As with the Berlin Wall, soldiers were ordered to fire on anyone caught crossing.

Israel has maintained control over Gaza's sea border and air space as well as local currency, electricity, fresh water, and trade. As a result, the International Court of Justice, various human rights groups, and European Union observers still consider Gaza under occupation. Desperate Palestinians dig tunnels under Gaza to smuggle in food and water and medicine.

From the Israeli government's point of view, Gaza remains a hotbed of terror. Hamas, which fights violently with rival faction Fatah, has used hospitals to stage its sorties. Rockets and mortar rounds fired from Gaza have struck Israeli civilians.

However: since 2008, Israeli forces armed with high-tech weaponry have clamped down on travel in and out of Gaza, cut fuel and power, killed hundreds and wounded thousands in retaliatory air strikes, and continued with a blockade that has inflicted critical supply shortages and, according to the Red Cross and a host of international observers, all but destroyed Gaza's economy. Tens of thousands there are homeless. Half of Gaza's residents are refugees.

In 2004, a thirteen-year-old Palestinian girl named Iman al-Hams was shot while crossing alone into a secure area. The official account stated that she walked toward an army post while carrying a school bag that might have contained a bomb. But a recording made of the incident tells a different tale: that she was identified as a "girl of about ten" seen walking away from the post back toward a refugee camp. "She's behind the embankment, scared to death." After a soldier shot her in the leg, the commander on site, "Captain R.," existed the post, approached her, and fired twice into her head and several times into her body. "Anything that's mobile, that moves in the zone, even if it's a three-year-old, needs to be killed," he was heard to say. The official response: minor disciplinary action.

In 2009, photographs showed evidence of phosphorus burns on Palestinians caught by yet another Israeli offensive. Phosphorus arms are banned by international law because they all but cremate their victims. The 155mm rounds were of American manufacture. Surgeons reported massive burns inflicted by an unidentified new weapon. That year Israeli doctors admitted to illegally removing corneas, skin, and heart valves from dead Palestinians without permission from their families.

A ghetto of poor refugees forbidden from leaving. High walls and watchful guards. Secretive tunneling underneath to relieve the hardship. Forbidden weapons that cremate. Harvesting of body parts. Children shot in cold blood. Families driven from their homes. Sound familiar?

One day in 2004 a Palestinian musician stopped at the Beit Iba checkpoint in the West Bank was compelled by Israeli soldiers to entertain them with his violin. The soldiers were filmed by the Israeli human rights group Machsom Watch. The army later claimed that they were searching the man for explosives, and that he played "of his own volition." Many in Israel and elsewhere shuddered at what this incident evoked: painful memories of Jewish concentration camp musicians forced to play classical music for their Nazi captors. In 2007, Palestinian violinist Ramzi Aburedwan was barred from entering the Gaza Strip even though he and the rest of his orchestra had secured permission in advance.

Given that so much of human history represents a replay of past trauma, none of this should surprise anyone. As a host of witnesses and survivors have observed, collective trauma echoes down the generations, recreating past injustices, inflicting new ones symbolic of the old, in replay after terrible replay of what Freud had named "the compulsion to repeat." Before Freud, Pierre Janet had noted this compulsion; one of his patients, Leonie, wept to recount that, a family member having drowned when she was young, her lost husband had recently suffered the same fate. For that reason depth psychology, which studies the unconscious aspects of what motivates and compels, began not in hysteria, but in tears. We recreate what still hurts.

This compulsion waxes strongest in those who have been persecuted and continue to see themselves as victims. To think of oneself as a victim is to remain in a chronic posture of suspicion, guardedness, paranoia—and rage.

Once in a position of power, the self-defining victim recreates the original traumatic event symbolically, but this time from a position of advantage. Unhealed, the former victim now assumes the role of persecutor. The bullied becomes the bully. The survivor turns executioner.

To stop this Ahab Complex, this cyclical alternation of victim and persecutor, the survivor must find ways to reenact the original trauma more consciously, perhaps ceremonially, and while doing so make peace with the internalized victimizer-within, mourn and let go of what was injured, killed, or savagely curtailed, and set aside the demonic mask laid over the original persecutor and face the woefully weak human being beneath it: a move apart from forgiveness, to be sure, but a necessary humanization without which the persecutor remains clothed in mythic potency and importance. Many were startled to see what a pathetic little man that "beast" and "devil" Adolf Eichmann was on the stand at Nuremberg: not a superhuman creature in the end, but a banal bureaucrat devoid of conscience following orders he never questioned.

Those who permanently identify themselves as victims indulge sooner or later in bouts of persecution.

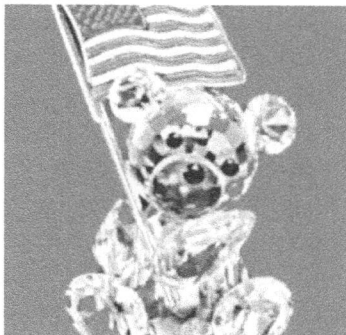

29 - 9/11:
The Fall of Pseudo-Innocence

It is a hallmark of pseudo-innocence to be shocked by the inevitable.

Part of the patriotic mythology of 9/11 is that the United States, bastion of freedom and stronghold of democracy, was struck with no warning for no reason. But decades of military meddling in the Middle East made a murderous counterblow certain. Americans whose style of life—namely, commodification and waste—creates poverty around the world looked up in shock to see the two towers fall. At Battery Park a growing mound of teddy bears served as a memorial of innocence struggling not to be shattered.

Some found it easier to pretend there had been no warning, not even from the CIA, although it had informed President Bush that terrorists planned to strike the U.S. with airliners. "All right, you've covered your ass now," he replied as he went back to planning the invasion of oil-rich Iraq. After the attacks, which were conducted by terrorists of Saudi nationality, American troops stood tense guard in front of the Saudi compound in Washington D.C. in case anyone but filmmaker Michael Moore made an embarrassing connection.

Largely unchallenged in the U.S., pseudo-innocence went on as, in exchange for the illusion of safety, hawks in red and blue neckties were offered whatever they wanted, from air time to Half Time, from billions in funding to most of the Bill of Rights. Political protesters were declared unpatriotic—an old tactic (see Chapters 20 and 25)—and borders were closed (Chapter 27) and laagered up tight. As fires cooled within the stricken metropolis, the ship of state went on battle alert against its own citizens (Chapter 21) while its forces streamed into the Persian Gulf once again at all ahead flank speed. Paranoia was no longer a dangerous derangement; overnight it had become a badge of honor, a certificate of loyalty, a political philosophy, a way of life. "The delusional," remarked Bill Moyers, "is no longer marginal." Time to call 911.

Oddly paired correspondences and synchronicities have joined emergency numbers, skyscrapers, fires, and red alerts around the globe since at least 1968, when the first phone ever to receive a 911 call was the red twin of another in Haleyville, Alabama. A fire closed the town's 911 museum in 1999. In Britain the emergency number is 999, and 111 in New Zealand, shooting location of a fantasy film in which two towers fell. 999 and 111: a fellowship of the ring. AT&T implemented "911" in 1968 after a fireman recommended it and two policemen tested it.

Shortly after 9/11, hotdog sellers near Ground Zero unknowingly stood under trees still shedding the ashes of human flesh—and this in a place whose first play, written by Robert Hunter and Lewis Morris and published in 1714, bore the title *Androborus* (The Man Eater). Soon the U.S. Government, like the figure of Cronus in Greek mythology, would assert its authority by eating its children, especially those of Arab descent or Muslim faith.

Although New York's reputation as an emblem of American ascendancy rose after the Civil War, the first fallen structures in the Empire City whose motto is *Excelsior*—"Ever Upward"—predate its American ownership. When the Dutch owned Manhattan (1624), a band of traders living on Indian foodstuffs grown on the elongated island's downward-pointing tip scrapped the plan for a fortress and erected instead a four-sided bastion of dirt a tenth the size of the original plan. Even so, in two years the foundations crumbled away, as though anticipating the futility of all such wealth-guarding projects from the outset. Infuriated, Peter Stuyvesant, New Amsterdam's director, complained to Holland that nothing he said or did could convince the settlers to strengthen their collapsed defenses or to quit helping themselves to souvenir stones from the sagging walls; nor did anyone there pause to reflect that, historically speaking, every heroically defended Ever Upward inevitably constellates an Eventually Downward.

Strengthening the walls would have done no good even in the short term. In eleven years the British and their seaborne artillery threatened the colony into submission; but the name of a dismantled palisade, the old fort's twin in hopeless defense, lingered in the lane running between Broadway and the East River: Wall Street, where one day the stock exchange would open on land once used to sell slaves and to inaugurate the nation's first president, the wealthiest landowner in Colonial America. William Kieft had ordered up the useless fortifications to protect his people from the Indians he had enraged, but the earth shifting underneath held to other priorities.

Ever Upward. Although the cityscape of today represents imperial ambition solidified in architecture, the word "skyscraper" recalls the billowing canvas-draped masts of incoming Europeans intent on gold and conquest. Towers, then, are economic topsails billowing above seas of international high finance in which almost anything can be bartered or bought—

including Manhattan, an Algonquian handle for "small island" or "hilly island," renamed New York in 1664 by the British after the powerful Catholic duke of that name. The Hudson River was named after a European captain facing arrest by the British and revocation of his trade mandate for flying Dutch colors illegally, like a pirate.

Given this weight and resonance of events, Radio City broadcast more on 9/11 than a terrorist attack planned and launched by hate-maddened zealots who murdered thousands of New Yorkers; more even than loss of liberties and marginalization of olive-skinned citizens in the name of state security. Not even the mound of memorial teddy bears could mask the underlying broadcast: that on 9/11, a shattering blow had been dealt to America's image of itself. From that day forward, even the most mindlessly patriotic, oblivious to the cost and weight and injustice of American dominance overseas, would pause at least once to ask, "Why do they hate us so much?"

Pseudo-innocence invites its own downfall.

30 - Katrina:
Nature Speaks Last

Since that first tenuous emergence of urbanization during the Fertile Crescent period of agricultural production, the tools and techniques of world-girdling civilization have grown large and clever enough to reshape what were once considered all-powerful deities: the sea, the sky, the rivers, and the land. Yet the first decade of the third millennium brought natural disasters of unprecedented strength: giant earthquakes in India, El Salvador, Nigeria, Kashmir, China, Iran, Haiti, and Chile; the worst heatwaves in known history, one killing thousands in Europe; a tsunami sweeping in on a quarter of a million of the doomed in Bangladesh, Burma, Maldives, Malaysia, Sri Lanka, India, and Thailand; an immense, deadly cyclone in Burma; the swine and bird flu epidemics....

In the United States, a series of powerful super-hurricanes begin crashing into the oil refineries of the Gulf of Mexico just as combat troops entered another Gulf, the Persian, to fight for oil. One of these storms was Katrina, the second strongest ever to strike the U.S. and the third deadliest. In the week before the storm hit New Orleans in 2005, the Bush administration was working to delete three words from the general principles of the United Nations: "respect for nature." *Mission accomplished.*

At one time New Orleans had been the most visibly significant urban region in the Deep South, at first as a hub of the slave trade, later as a key commerce port on the Gulf Coast. As an income gap yawned between whites and blacks, parts of the city fell into geographical depression as wells pumped petroleum from the ground. By the time Katrina rolled in, swamps and low-lying former marshes cleared for inhabitation sat below sea level: a full 49% of the city protected only by shoddy levees built by the Army Corps of Engineers. When they broke in multiple places, most of the city flooded. With so much of the vegetation that had once ringed New Orleans cut away or eroded, storm surge reached inland for many miles.

Many people evacuated, but some were too poor, elderly, or sick to leave. (25% of the pre-Katrina population lived below the poverty line.) No evacuation provisions were made for them. As bodies floated in the streets, state and federal emergency teams slowly made their way into the city. Under Michael Brown, the Federal Emergency Management Agency actually turned away trucks, buses, the Coast Guard, Amtrak, the U.S. Forest Service, and numerous local and international offers of assistance in order to keep things "coordinated." Later, FEMA's emergency trailers were found to leak formaldehyde fumes.

President Bush returned from his Texas vacation a full day after the disaster and flew over New Orleans in a helicopter: "You're doing a heck of a job, Brownie!" Vice President Cheney personally intervened, but only to send power crews to Collins, Mississippi to keep gasoline and diesel fuel flowing in the Colonial Pipeline. The startled crews had been busy restoring electricity to two local hospitals. As hundreds of police fled the drowned city, soldiers of the Mississippi and Louisiana National Guard watched the dismal news helplessly from Iraq. Guard units from other states were delayed for days until the official approval to move in was finally cleared.

Historically speaking, this is how it looks when an empire falls apart, when the absurdity of mismanagement becomes so blatant that it speaks for itself. 9/11: "Red alert!" The depressed Big Easy: "The party's over."

This time, however, more than an empire is falling. From New Orleans back to the *Titanic*, from melting polar caps to islands of floating plastic, an entrenched disregard of the presence of the natural world has wreaked such damage on the biosphere that we find ourselves threatened by the same mass extinction now annihilating species across the world. In many cases the damage was not deliberate; in most, it stemmed from the strange hubristic notion that we know better than Earth does how to run the laws of nature.

It is increasingly, painfully clear, however, that no top-down, machine-minded, fear-driven bureaucracy can hope to manage such living complexities, let alone comprehend them. We learn interesting lessons, however, when we pause to study how nature manages things.

We have learned, for example, that many animals besides us use tools; that whales sing songs of a harmonic sophistication comparable to that of human music; that dolphins include human fishers in their mutually supportive fishing strategies; that magpies, elephants, and other animals remember dead loved ones and engage in what look like rituals of mourning; that lions and wolves pretend not to notice nearby game until they feel safe enough to eat it; that mice feel empathy for the pain of other mice. The real surprise in all this is not that other animals possess such rich capabilities for consciousness, but how long it has taken us to realize that no firm line separates us from our fellow creatures. In many ways, fish taught us sailing, birds flying, wolves tracking, spiders weaving, horses and other pack animals how to traverse a landscape. Our cars still resemble them, with eyes in front and wheels for legs.

Grasping this, the field of biomimicry makes conscious, creative use of some of nature's design principles. A spider weaves a web hundreds of times stronger per unit of material than steel, which requires labors and temperatures the spider need not bother about. Why not weave steel her way? Architects are designing tall buildings to be as strong and naturally self-cooled as termite mounds. Echo-location, used by bats and dolphins to navigate, will soon help the blind to walk. The underlying logic makes sense: Why reinvent what nature has already experimented with for billions of years?

Walk on any stretch of fertile ground and you will find yourself walking on a carpet of invisible fungi. Its fruiting bodies (reproductive organs) appear to us as mushrooms. We eat some of them, avoid others, extract penicillin from still others, but only lately have scientists begun to grasp even a little of the intricacy spun through an inch or two of topsoil. Communicating with itself through chemical messengers much as a human brain does, fungi manage entire ecosystems. Cover a tree to prevent it from photosynthesizing until it weakens, and the fungi below it, sensing this, divert nutrients from other trees to fortify the shaded one.

This mycelial wisdom reaches across entire continents to form intricate networks characterized by rich nodes of organic connectivity: just one control system employed by the planetary organism to remain in balance. Since 1971, James Lovelock and Lynn Margulis have hypothesized that Earth's entire surface, including oceans and atmosphere, seeks to maintain itself in a state of regulated hospitality to life, a global feat made ever more difficult by poorly regulated industry and urban sprawl.

If our efforts since the Fertile Crescent (Chapter 1) demonstrate anything at all, it's that, despite our relative success in modifying our surroundings here and there, we cannot win the war against nature, any more than we can win one against our own nature. *We are* nature, dust to dust, going forth on two legs under a big brain wired to a voicebox. Our nerves recall mycelia, our eyes shine like globes of sea water, our hands and feet splay like tree and river branches. The very word "human" derives from "humus."

We can, if we choose, delight in Earth's complexity, appreciate its beauty, dip our experimental brushes into its palette, even bend it where it's flexible to better serve human needs; but we cannot war upon it without suffering ever more dire consequences as its creatures, storms, and eruptions from below remind us ever and again of what Katrina brought ashore: the unavoidable *truth* (from a word for "tree") that the escalating costs of believing ourselves masters of the natural world are far too high to sustain.

Nature always has the last word, and we ignore its intelligence at our peril.

Coda:
What Works, Enlivens,
Reconciles, and Endures?

In the compost of history's ignored but crucial lessons await the seeds of what we can do differently.

Consider our list:

1. Human nature is cast as warlike and depraved primarily by those who benefit from repressive programs to control it.
2. Empires are inherently unsustainable and eventually self-destruct.
3. Changing or replacing a few elements, even key ones at the top, seldom exerts deep or lasting change on a broken system.
4. Inner work separated from outer action hands over the outer world to ambitious "realists" who seize the hard seats of power and authority.
5. Long-term repression only strengthens the repressed.
6. An absolutist emphasis on an invisible heaven paves the way for hellish results to disorder this world.
7. Any culture that allows the mistreatment of children sets itself up to be conquered by them.
8. Denial kills.

9. No matter what social pressures are brought to bear, we all retain the capacity to rise above our time when higher obligations demand it.
10. Adapt or die.
11. Scientific knowledge provides welcome verification but has never been humanity's sole means of knowing.
12. Sooner or later, chronic self-hatred enlarges into hatred of humanity, of scapegoats, and ultimately of the world.
13. Clinging conservatively to traditional procedures, rites, and rituals instead of renewing them hastens cultural decline.
14. Violence always ignites more violence.
15. Systems and theories that shrink human nature to its material components eventually take on the trappings of unconscious evangelism.
16. Leaving positions of power unwatched and unregulated leaves them vulnerable to capture by unbalanced minds obsessed with control.
17. Using mechanical, linear, single-solution thinking to fix a complex living system almost always further destabilizes it.
18. The weed seeds of reform imposed from above or brought from outside sprout into new forms of oppression.
19. In any conflict between opposing groups, the strongest mythology always wins.
20. When organized extremists make an extra-legal bid for total power, their excuse is always the same: state security.
21. Those who level paranoid accusations harbor a toxic rage that undermines social structures the accusers say they support.
22. The talented exiled by the arrogant and ignorant often returns, but as a dangerous enemy.
23. Ignoring the monsters within us enlarges them exter-

nally into gigantic, dangerous creations.

24. To find resolution, deep hurts and conflicts must be lived through consciously until they reveal how constant fiddling stops them from healing themselves.
25. Spreaders of intimidation, slander, and fear grow louder until they are seen through and denounced.
26. Those who call loudest for eliminating egotism are themselves most in need of their message.
27. Oppressive borders invite their own transgression.
28. Those who permanently identify themselves as victims indulge sooner or later in bouts of persecution.
29. Pseudo-innocence invites its own downfall.
30. We ignore nature's intelligence at our peril.

That's what hasn't worked, but what has? Here is the list reimagined and restated as lessons learned:

1. A knowledgeable basic faith in the constructive possibilities of human nature encourages forms of government and education that help our nature to unfold and realize itself.
2. Sustainable forms of human community have thrived since the dawn of humanity and are continuing to all over the world.
3. Systems nearing the edge of chaos can be reconfigured relatively quickly if the visions guiding their interactions are free to evolve.
4. Humanity's greatest practical visionaries demonstrate that inner work and outer change go seamlessly together and support each other.
5. Repression only strengthens the drive for liberty forming the core of who and what we are.
6. Cultural groups whose members experience the world as sacred and ensouled tend to cherish, protect, and learn from it.
7. Cultures that genuinely care for their children, raising

them in an atmosphere of abundance and fearlessness, can look forward to adding their health and talent to the living hearth of the community.

8. Paying heed to the thoughtful messengers of unpleasant news has often saved us from having to face irreversible disaster.

9. Our era does not make us: we make it if we choose to actively participate in what goes on around us.

10. Successful adaptation means keeping our balance within changing conditions without losing our sense of ourselves, individually or collectively.

11. Scientific knowledge allows an invaluable check on the accuracy of our perceptions so long as those perceptions remain free to operate in trust and self-confidence.

12. Those who genuinely accept themselves tend to accept others and to enjoy the world as well.

13. Creatively used, our traditions, lore, and rites of passage can inform us on how to adapt to a changing world, accepting what's new and valuable while prizing what endures.

14. Peaceful assertiveness has a way of spreading itself around.

15. Awe and humility of the mystery of human becoming can guard us against the blinders of reductive dogmatism and the fear of our own nature.

16. Carefully monitoring positions of power can help prevent their seizure by psychologically immature, uninitiated people filled with fear and ambition.

17. Complex living systems challenge us to think about flow, adaptation, networking, and consequences instead of rushing forward with unhelpful fixes or pseudo-solutions.

18. True reform evolves a person, group, or system from within, with full participation by every member of the whole.

19. In any conflict between opposing groups, tending the most comprehensive, mutually assembled picture of aims and goals diminishes division and increases change and hope.

20. The most secure state is the one in which people have real control over how well they are fed, clothed, educated, and heard.

21. The more democratic and lively and productive a society, the less need it has to scapegoat anyone.

22. Talented individuals whose ideas are listened to are the same people whose experiments and innovations move the rest of us in new directions.

23. Remaining mindful of the monsters within not only guards against externalizing them unconsciously, it transmutes them into useful helpers and bringers of psychic energy.

24. Allowing the healing forces of mind and body to do their work with minimal interference fosters greater self-trust and dilutes the fear of being out of control.

25. Cohesive cultural groups tend not to raise bullies, but when it happens anyway, they let bullies know that deliberately slanderous or otherwise divisive remarks or actions are not welcome.

26. Genuine self-respect combined with close relationships of mutual support and deep caring diminish narcissism.

27. Tearing down walls around coalitions, neighborhoods, or nations coincides with tearing them down around the over-defended heart.

28. Those who outgrow the victim role also outgrow the persecutor role.

29. Critical attention to the true costs and consequences of our way of life moves us out of being infantile spectators of the world into an adult sense of active, responsible, international citizenship.

30. Working appreciatively with nature's intelligence

**transforms exploitation and alienation into partner-
ship and homecoming.**

In times like ours, when the deep structures of how we
think about ourselves and the world shift just below the hori-
zons of awareness, an apocalyptic tone filters thoughts about
what lies ahead. Frightened people who forget the panics of
1000 and 2000 buy batteries and beef jerky before the the
clock strikes 2012 and dies of some cosmic alignment or other.
The reflective wonder if the End of Times misanthropy of religious fundamentalism will bring about a self-fulfilling end of
the world as human life has known it. Will Earth's fever break,
or will it overheat us all?

It is entirely possible that our species will not survive the
historical crucible in which war, corporatization, climate
change, ecological destruction, mass extinction, religious
extremism, and Promethean enthusiasm concoct a toxic brew
too poisonous to digest easily. But our lists support another
possibility: that what is ending is not the world, but a worldview, one that limits what is real to what can be bought, sold,
or measured; that sells human possibility short; that institutionalizes paranoia and competition; that gives religion permission to be as warlike and intolerant as its least mature
adherents could ever wish; that installs and deifies a perma-
nent ruling class; that instills helplessness, anomie, and cynicism in entire populations; that ecocidally consumes, transforms, and wastes earthly minerals, soils, and ecosystems upon
whose failing health we all depend.

Built on cultural, scientific, economic, political, and spiritual foundations that once seemed solid, this Big Machine par-
adigm shaping so much of what we feel, think, and do looks
on second thought to be grinding to a stop, or even toppling
like a tower whose heady gigantism has eclipsed itself.

If historical examples demonstrate the transience of titanic
structures handed over to entropy by hubris, coldness, poverty
of imagination, and stupidity, they also make clear that times

of rupture allow new forms to surface from depths previously concealed: fertile ground for planting fresh innovations in how to live with each other and our planet in communities more truly grown from the seed of our best-dreamed aspirations.

Perhaps any culture we survive to create will be sane and sound and sustainable over the long haul only insofar as it turns the lessons of the past to discovery of what works well in the present in service to a fulfilling future.

www.ingramcontent.com/pod-product-compliance
Lightning Source LLC
Chambersburg PA
CBHW020949030426
42339CB00004B/20

9 780982 627907